ONWARD THROUGH hell

COMPANY L OF MENOMINEE - 125TH INFANTRY REGIMENT 32ND DIVISION - AT HILL 212 IN WORLD WAR I

BY ROSS PARCELS

To Kelly & Carolyn — Thanks for reminding me that the mistakes are O.K.

Ross Parcels

Library of Congress Control Number: 2007940744
ISBN 10: 0976009390
ISBN 13: 9780976009399

Published by Aurora Books
Aurora Books, 625 First Street, Menominee, Michigan 49858
Designed and printed by Hahn Printing Incorporated
752 North Adams Road, Eagle River, Wisconsin 54521

First Edition, First Printing

To the Memory of Company L

Acknowledgments

Thanks to Frank Kellerman of Brown University, Philip Bantin, Indiana University, Terry Cook, University of Manitoba, Eliot Wilczek, Tufts University, Sandra Wiles, Phoenix Art Museum, and Jeffrey Schultz. All made significant contributions to the thesis project from which this book is derived.

In addition, thank you to all who helped me gather research materials from and at many repositories around the country, including but not limited to: Mitchell Yockelson, reference archivist at the National Archives at College Park, and Jeffery Hartley, Chief Librarian at the National Archives; Dr. Art Bergeron, United States Military History Insitute, Carlisle, Pennsylvania; the Outreach Library staff at the University of Illinois; the staff at Spies Library in Menominee, Michigan; the staff at the Menominee County Historical Society's Michael J. Anuta Research Center, especially Janet Callow and Eileen Hannot-Tork; and my friend, William Milz.

I am grateful to the Graduate School of Library and Information Science, University of Illinois, whose financial support during 2005-2006 through the awarding of a Hearsey Fellowship enabled me to continue my library school studies and write the thesis.

Most importantly, my heartfelt thanks to my wife, Linda C. Murto, and to Linda C. Smith, University of Illinois at Urbana-Champaign. Without them, this book would not have been written.

Contents

Preface

Onward Through Hell comprises three essays from a thesis I wrote under the auspices of the Graduate School of Library and Information Science at the University of Illinois at Urbana-Champaign entitled (Hell Forgotten and Remembered: Essays on Menominee's Company L and Hill 212 in Memory, History, and the Archives.) As this title implies, my original concerns were not purely historical. In order to now focus more closely on local history — and not coincidentally because words are cheap in academe but dear to the self-publisher — I have made significant, even wholesale, cuts in the text of that thesis. Some of the flavor of the thesis remains, however, since changes to two of the remaining three essays were minor and the third essay was expanded. This book, then, centers on Company L of Menominee, Michigan, during their very first day of battle at Hill 212 in World War I, the propaganda and news in Menominee around the time of that event, and the aftermath of that battle, including the burial and reburial(s) of the nine soldiers from Menominee in Company L who were killed on July 31, 1918.

Future researchers have the opportunity to build on what I have done, should they wish to do so, and to make right any lacunae I may have left by accident or design.

From Preface to University of Illinois Thesis

While researching and writing this thesis, I visited a number of different storehouses: the local Menominee, Michigan, archives, museum, and library; the National Archives; the Military History Institute; and other libraries and archival institutions of all sizes. The variety of materials in these repositories helped me to learn about memory, history, and the archives, and forged a protean dynamic that kept this project fresh. The learning does not stop when I put these words on the page; I am certain that next week's try would be different from this one. As you will read, absolute answers have eluded me, just as the perfect archive and set of documents that would have told all have done.

While studying and reading about Company L and Hill 212, I came to several different conclusions about what had actually occurred. As I visited different repositories and discovered different sources, my views on the battle changed. I would write things one way, creating history just as archivists and curators create memory. Then I would have to start over. It really does not matter in historical terms: from a certain point-of-view, Company L played a minor part in both the Aisne-Marne offensive and in the American Expeditionary Forces' (AEF) trials in World War I. Even within the scope of Company L' s first day of battle that I attempt to describe, it could be said that not much happened. The 32nd Division, 63rd Brigade, 125th Regiment, and 3rd Battalion, really did not get very far on their first (and even second) day of battle. Division, Brigade, Regiment, Battalion, and Company L were battered but not beaten. Thirty-three men from Company L alone were killed during that first day. A few days later, the men of the 32nd Division had chased to the Vesle River a German army that chose to retreat and were stymied there subsequent to being relieved. End of story.

But the residue of the battle lingers on in memory and records. This was a local company's first assault. Much occurred that was emblematic of wars in general and this one in particular: surprise, death, perhaps trickery, and panic, fear, bravery. Rarely do I delve into the problems that the entire AEF faced in World War I, but I want to reiterate here that what happened to Company L was common. It is significant that what happened to Company L was so typical.

So what really did happen and how will the battle be remembered in the future? That is what drove me over and again to look at the events of July 31 afresh. That is why it was important to me to try to find an answer — even if that answer is incomplete or even partially incorrect or not to be discovered.

Essay 1

Menominee Men at Hill 212: July 31, 1918

Nine men from Menominee in Michigan's Upper Peninsula, soldiers in Company L, were killed in one horrific day of fighting in France during World War I.

"It was onward through Hell," wrote Company L Corporal Harry Allard after he had lived through a week at the front.[1] And for the soldiers of Company L of Menominee, formerly a National Guard unit, their initial assault on July 31, 1918, was certainly the most hellish of them all.

The men of Company L, 3rd Battalion, 125th Infantry Regiment, endured their baptism-of-fire as a lead unit in the 32nd (Red Arrow) Division's attack on the German machine gun nests in the fields and woods at Hill 212. The action took place near the villages of Sergy and Cierges[2], a few miles from Chateau-Thierry, well within long-range shelling distance of Paris.

Despite having his nose grazed by a German bullet in a later fight, Harry Allard survived the war.[3] Oliver Allard of Company L, Harry's brother, also survived, and by war's end had risen to the rank of second lieutenant. But Sergeants John Teichler and Harold Johnson; Corporals Walter Pada, John Stauber, and Peter Boivin; Mechanic Fred St. Peter; and Privates William Baker and Arthur Lueskow: these Company L soldiers from Menominee died in their first day of battle.[4] Company L Corporal Albert Johnson of Menominee was also killed in the attack, although there was some confusion in his case. Part of the mix-up occurred because Albert's brother, Anton, another Company L soldier who had been transferred to Company H, 128th Infantry, was also killed in action just a few days later.[5]

In fact, the entire Menominee company was hit hard during July 31 and the following week. Company L's first assault echoed that of other American troops in 1918: soldiers stumbled blindly into the whirl of war and paid for their inexperience.[6] Once engaged in battle, though, the men from Menominee fought bravely and, to a degree, effectively.[7]

Company L's assault on Hill 212 took place during the Second Battle of the Marne or the Aisne-Marne offensive, an operation that was a "turning point of World War I."[8] German forces had, during one of their several desperate offensives of spring, 1918, pushed as far as Chateau-Thierry on the Marne River, just fifty-six miles from Paris.[9] In so doing, the Germans had forged a salient. Now, German General Erich Ludendorff went on the offensive again, attacking the Reims salient in Champagne on July 15 in an effort to break through. As Tim Travers writes, "time was now critical," for in addition to the 20 huge American divisions already on French soil, "more American troops were pouring into Europe at the rate of 250,000 per month."[10] The German army needed to attack before their numerical superiority slipped away and while their artillery strength held.

French intelligence had warned of an attack and German movements telegraphed it: there was no surprise. The German army was stopped cold and from this time until war's end the French would be on the offensive. On July 18 the French counterattacked on a wide front and attempted with vigor to eliminate the Marne salient. The United States divisions that fought in the Aisne-Marne action were attached to the French army; in particular, the 32nd Division and Company L fought as part of the 38th Corps of the French 6th Army.[11] The French and Americans steadily pushed the German troops back. As General Robert Lee Bullard put it, "Out of the Chateau-Thierry salient the enemy was going, but he was going stubbornly — turning ever and anon like a wounded lion upon his assailant."[12] Into this fierce fight and onto the world stage were thrust the men from the Red Arrow Division and Menominee's Company L.

National Guard regiments from Michigan and Wisconsin, incorporated into the army following the United States declaration of war in 1917, formed the bulk of the two large brigades (the 63rd and 64th, respectively) that made up the 32nd Division. During the Aisne-Marne campaign, the Red Arrow Division earned the laudatory nickname that the French gave them: "Les Terribles."[13] The division fought well during the American Expeditionary Forces' (AEF) brief and bloody stay in France, which produced an estimated 114,000-126,000 American deaths in roughly two hundred days of fighting.[14] It can be difficult to discern just *how* well the division fought but note, for example, historian David Trask's objective assessment of AEF troops attached to the French 6th Army in the context of his gloss on the overall effect of the AEF in the war:

> Although the US army never attained the decisive victory envisaged for it, the overall American reinforcement provided the margin of victory. . . . Ironically some of the best combat service came from American divisions temporarily assigned to allied forces, especially those attached to the French 6th [including the 32nd Division] and 10th armies during the Aisne-Marne offensive. . . .[15]

Local Context

The units that the Red Arrow Division comprised were closely linked with the towns and cities of Michigan and Wisconsin whose men had filled the ranks of the pre-war National Guard companies and regiments. Prior to 1917, Menominee's Company L had formed part of the 33rd Infantry Regiment in the Michigan National Guard: at least some of the Menominee soldiers killed on July 31 were buried with the National Guard insignia still on their uniform collars.[16] The war changed these units drastically: drafts and transfers not only increased their size, but gave these local companies a national flavor quite different from their earlier social club atmosphere.[17] Also, men from Menominee County did not necessarily join Company L. They served throughout the AEF, or even, in rare cases, enlisted with the armed forces of England or Canada. All told, out of a company of around 200-215 soldiers, only an estimated 55-60 Menominee men went into battle with Company L on July 31.[18]

In fact, in a strange twist of events, even Company L's longtime commander served with a different unit during the war. Oscar Falk, Menominee's portly 53 year-old postal clerk, had been Company L's commander for more than a decade. Falk had departed with the company for training in Waco, Texas, but had been declared unfit for combat and relieved of his command. He then traveled to Washington to plead his case, was re-examined, and placed at the head of Company F of Alpena in the 2nd Battalion of the 125th Infantry.[19]

On July 31, Captain Falk, weakened with illness, commanded Company F in battle; Falk got his wish to fight, as F Company led the 2nd Battalion's assault on the woods known as les Jomblets at Hill 212. There, his company was, in the words of a company history from the same battalion, "almost annihilated,"[20] and Falk himself was mortally wounded by shellfire "while he was relaying a message over the telephone during the din of battle."[21]

Falk's longtime lieutenant, Merritt "Tug" Wilson of Menominee, who had transferred from Company L to Company F at his commander's behest, wrote: "They found that a piece of shell had hit him in the leg and travled [sic] up and entered the abdomen."[22] The Captain had been brought to the field hospital in shock and with a severe leg wound, a "compound comminuted fracture of the femur," remembered the surgeon who had operated on him.[23] Despite the seriousness of Falk's condition, the doctor speculated that Falk might have survived; instead, "the [field] hospital was bombed by the German aviators and after that they turned their machine guns on us. . . . The hospital had to [be] closed and the patients evacuated."[24] Falk died on August 1.[25] A veteran of the Spanish-American War and, perhaps, Company L's strongest link to its pre-World War I past, Falk was killed leading men he had not known before the war.

Still, despite the break-up of the old company, L's ties to Menominee remained strong; so strong that after the company departed for training in Waco in October 1917, the local daily, the *Menominee Herald-Leader* and, indeed, the citizens of Menominee, continued to regard the company as theirs.

Moving Up to the Front

Company L veteran Oliver Allard of Menominee made a simple but important observation in a brief account of his wartime service: the Americans, for the most part, were not engaged in trench warfare as the Allies (Entente) and Central Powers had been for most of the war. "Our hardiest encounters," remembered Allard, "were on open terrain, hills, valleys, and woods."[26] Such was the character of the July 31 fight.

During the night of July 30-31, two battalions of the Michigan brigade (63rd) of the Red Arrow Division moved into the front line next to the division's Wisconsin brigade (64th), who had gone over the top earlier that day. Just which two battalions and their placement on the line is something of a mystery in the sources, but it may be an important one to explore. First, the question appears to bear directly on the fighting that occurred on July 31; second, it demonstrates both how confused the participants and their memories were and the disagreement in the record over even a relatively straightforward matter.

According to the *32nd Division: Summary of Operations in the World War*, "the new front was occupied by the 1st and 2nd Battalions, 125th Infantry, from right to left."[27] This was indeed the case despite some assertions to the contrary. According to this source, Company L and the rest of the 3rd Battalion of the 125th, including Companies I, K, and M, spent that evening "in Bois de la Garenne, 500 meters west of Courmont" — and to the rear of the 1st and 2nd Battalions.[28] This account is corroborated, in substance if not in every detail, in Company I Sergeant Lyle Cole's diary: "We go to the front in support that night . . . back of the village of Ciergies. . . . The next morning [prior to the attack] we . . . took up positions along St. Martin Road, west of Ciergies."[29]

"History of Company 'G'" — Company G was in the 2nd Battalion, 125th

Infantry — tells another story: "The relief [of the 28th Division] was made. . . . The Third Battalion of the 125th Infantry was on our left and the 127th Infantry [64th Brigade] on the right."[30] This was indeed where the 3rd Battalion ended up by order during the battle: to the left (west) of the 2nd Battalion. It is not where the 3rd Battalion was placed during the night, and is, as well, misleading as to the relative positions of the 2nd and 1st Battalions.

"Report on Operations," the divisional report on the Second Battle of the Marne, observed that the 63rd Brigade of the 32nd Division relieved the 28th Division and took its place on the left of the 64th Brigade, 32nd Division, but did not give details.[31] The "Consolidated Operations Report" from August 14, 1918, stated that "The front line . . . was held by the three battalions of the 125th Infantry" [each battalion with a machine gun company].[32] The *32nd Division in the World War* noted that "the Michigan soldiers [of the 1st and 2nd Battalions] duplicated the feat of their Wisconsin comrades on the night before by making a successful relief in the face of trying circumstances," but did not explain further.[33]

In truth, the Michigan men were confused. The following message from a company in the 1st Battalion in Company L's regiment, the 125th Infantry, to the captain of a Wisconsin company in the 127th Infantry of the 64th Brigade, received in the early morning of July 31, demonstrates just how difficult a task the relief of the 28th Division turned out to be:

> From 3rd. Plat., Co. C, 125th Inf. — To the platoon on my right. We came up into this strip of the woods last night in relief of the 110th. We are not fully oriented as yet and any dope you can give me as to your outfit, orders, intentions, etc. would help considerably in getting our bearings. Please draw a small sketch showing just what part of this country is ours and which is enemy. By the way, what are those Frenchmen doing out in front? Signed J. Brown, 2nd. Lt., 125th. Inf.[34]

This message places the 1st Battalion of the 125th Infantry squarely on the right (east) of the 63rd Brigade. Later on July 31, when Major General William Haan, commanding the 32nd Division, ordered an attack, the 1st Battalion of the 125th Infantry was partially in the 64th Brigade's sector, which was to the right (east) of the 63rd. Haan ordered that "by conference between brigade commanders, arrangements will be made to gradually withdraw elements now in the sector of the 64th Brigade to be replaced by elements from the latter brigade."[35] He added that "this can probably be done during the advance."[36]

Haan later wrote: "I decided to attack on the entire front, directing the brigade on the left [the 63rd] to push forward, echeloning its troops on the right [the 1st Battalion] to the rear."[37] The decision to withdraw the 125th Infantry's 1st Battalion from the front line and place it in support of the 2nd Battalion on the right (east), and to bring up the 3rd Battalion, under Major Charles Mathews, to attack on the left (west), may have caused further confusion during the ensuing battle.[38]

July 31

Wednesday, July 31, found the Michigan brigade, the 63rd, and Wisconsin men (64th Brigade) of the Red Arrow Division side-by-side, from left to right, west to east. The 2nd Battalion of the 63rd was on the left of that brigade and the 1st was on the right. To the left of the 63rd was the 42nd (Rainbow) Division.[39] To the right of the 64th were the French. Oliver Allard of Menominee and Company L remembered, "It was a hot sunny day."[40] "In front of the 32nd," according to the division's history, "loomed Hill 212 above the village of Cierges, a hornet's nest of German machine guns."[41] Company L was about to attack those guns.

The divisional history set the scene: "Directly in front of us was the long, open slope of the Ourcq Valley, reaching to the small woods leading up to the woods of Les Jomblettes [sic] on Hill 212. . . . This objective constituted one of the strongest German positions on the line of the Ourcq [River]."[42] The

Michigan brigade and Company L were to assault the woods on Hill 212 known as les Jomblets, the Bois de la Planchette and, as a final objective, the Bois Pelger. Facing them were elements of the German VII Army, VIII Reserve Corps.[43]

Field Orders No. 11 from 63rd Brigade Headquarters were issued at 12:45 p.m., just over an hour before the attack on Hill 212 was expected to take place: "The advance will be made with two Battalions, the 2nd and 3rd Bns. [including Company L] 125th Infantry in the first line," the orders read. The orders also dictated that "The 1st Bn. 125th Infantry will maintain its present position until our first and second lines have passed when it will form as a third line battalion in rear of our right."[44]

Oliver Allard wrote, "The 'zero hour' was 2:00 P.M." The *32nd Division Summary of Operations* noted that "In the 63d Infantry Brigade, the attack started shortly after 2:00 p.m."[45] Upon his return to Menominee in February, 1919, Corporal John Daley of Company L remembered that the order to attack was given "around 2:30."[46] Lyle Cole, from Company I of the 3rd Battalion, corroborated this: "At 2:30 p.m. we went over the top."[47] "History of Company 'G'" stated "that the action was to commence at two o'clock in the afternoon, but through some error of mishandling, the Second Battalion [125th Infantry] received the order fifteen minutes after the action was supposed to have commenced."[48] According to this source, then, the 2nd Battalion did not go into action until just around 3:00 p.m. Captain Emil Gansser of the 126th Infantry noted that "some battalion commanders did not receive the attack orders until after the zero hour."[49] Around 7:00 p.m., the talented leader of the 2nd Battalion, Major Guy Wilson, sent a terse rejoinder to Colonel William Morrow, commander of the 125th Infantry: "Order received 2:10 to be executed at 2:00 p.m. The delay [in carrying out the] order [because it was] not received until after action started."[50]

Oliver Allard recalled: "Men fixed their bayonets," and then, "When the command was given by Captain John McCabe, the men followed an artillery barrage."[51] Cole remembered in his diary that "we went . . . through a ripe wheat field, pass through a German birage which dug deep holes in the soft ground. . . . Beyond that birage we came to the Orco River about 3' wide."[52] We jumped a small stream known as the Ourcq River," Allard wrote, "and in the wheat field ahead we were confronted by the enemy who were surprised as well as us."[53]

According to orders, recounted Daley, upon advancing Company L "would pass two lines of Americans before we hit upon any Germans."[54] A reading of Field Orders No. 11 (63rd Brigade) reveals directions that were probably (and apparently) easily misunderstood when relayed: a complicated set of marching orders coupled with a perhaps overly-simplified approach to the task of dislodging the Germans from their positions on Hill 212.[55] On the left of the 63rd Brigade's line, the 3rd Battalion of the 125th Infantry Regiment, which comprised Company L along with Companies I, K, and M, advanced in a northeasterly direction against Hill 212 near Sergy[56]; the 2nd Battalion of the 125th was to take Cierges and attempt a frontal assault on les Jomblets. Daley's comment that Company L expected to meet lines of American troops and field messages during the battle to the effect that the 3rd Battalion had seen no "friendly troops north of Sergy"[57] : these imply that in whatever manner the orders had been relayed, they had not been fully understood.

In any event, as a lead element in the assault on Hill 212, the 3rd Battalion and Company L might have expected to meet with enemy resistance sooner rather than later. But just as clearly, communication had broken down prior to the advance to the degree that some soldiers in the 3rd Battalion did not even know they were leading the attack. Lyle Cole of Company I recalled: "We had seen men on the side of Hill #212 get up and go up the hill and disappear over the top. We were cheering them on thinking they were the first wave. The [American] machine gunners [at the Ourcq] informed us they were Germans and we were in the first wave. This was news to us."[58]

Meanwhile, Company L drifted toward the German positions. "We crossed a field of wheat," Corporal Daley continued, " . . . and were advancing towards the road which bounded this field on the north. We kept looking for two lines of Americans. . . . There was no sign of them, and no battle raged, with the exception of a stray shell occasionally."[59]

One such stray killed Corporal Peter Boivin of Menominee. "We just got into action," Daley recalled, "and advanced about 50 yards, when he [Boivin] was struck directly in the head with a shell."[60] Prior to the battle, Boivin had been waiting for a letter from his wife with a photograph of her and the couple's newborn child, but the mail had not arrived in time.[61]

Joseph Stauber of Menominee was wounded in the cheek, neck, and back, by machine gun and shell fire early in the fight. Upon returning home ahead of his unit, in January 1919, he was hailed a "Menominee Hero" in headlines in the *Herald-Leader*. "I received three wounds," Stauber explained, "but do not remember just how they come. . . . My first wound . . . temporarily paralyzed me."[62]

After lying on the ground for some time, Stauber managed to drag himself "about 500 yards" where he rested at an embankment. "A comrade came up and told me that I was bleeding," Stauber told the *Herald-Leader*. "I said I knew it, and had been shot in the neck. He told me that the worst wound was in the back. He helped me with first aid, ripping off my shirt, and I had a wound in my back larger than my hand." For Joseph Stauber, the war was over.[63]

When Company L, moving ahead cautiously, neared a road at the north end of the wheat field through which they were advancing, Corporal Daley told the *Herald-Leader*, they came upon a clump of bushes. "Suddenly," recalled Daley, "11 Germans jumped up from behind the bush, hands in the air, one waving a white flag, and shouting 'mercy comrade.' Lieut. [Charles] Hammond, who was second in command, a sergeant and two privates went over to the Germans, searched them, and sent them to the rear."[64] This part of Daley's account was apparently corroborated in essence in a field message sent shortly after 5:00 p.m.: "Eight prisoners taken by Company L. 125th here now."[65]

While the German prisoners may have been safe, Company L teetered on the edge of danger. "We were all standing there looking and joking about the . . . prisoners," continued Daley, "when suddenly the 'pop-pop' of the machines [sic] guns were heard. . . . The woods just across the road, of which we were within 30 yards, were filled with machine gun nests. They [the Germans] were everywhere, up in the trees, under the brush, all over."[66] Oliver Allard wrote, "Our fire downed many but their machine gun fire from the top of the hill stopped our advances for awhile."[67] At 4:25, a message was sent from Company L's battalion: "Held up on account of machine gun fire north of [Caranda] mill."[68]

Allard may have remembered, in some way, the surrender incident many years later when he wrote: "We were confronted by the enemy who were surprised as well as us." Surrender itself was a tricky issue in World War I. It could cost a soldier his life, for one thing. Bogus surrender was a common tactic in the war, and it is quite possible that the German "surrender" to Company L had been planned. In any case, the bigger surprise obviously belonged to Company L. "We were immediately sent into the fray," Daley remembered, "and that's where we lost heavily. There were 42 men killed, and 100 wounded by the time night came."[69]

For 3rd Battalion platoon leader Robert Horine, the battle was much more elemental. He remembered crossing the Ourcq, and then moving "straight up Hill 212, through wheat fields, halfway up the first Boche barrage dropped on us and machine guns opened up from every point of the compass; men were hit, hesitated, dropped, but the lines moved forward."[70] Emil Gansser wrote that the 3rd Battalion's assault "was made over exposed ground covered by enemy fire from this hill [212], Jomblets Woods, and the town of Cierges."[71] Horine recalled that "A three hour fight for the hill followed, a fight which then seemed to me, and still seems like a fight against tremendous odds, a fight which near its close was almost a fight without weapons."[72]

As Company L continued to attack, recalled Daley, "the way men were falling was awful."[73] Daley saw Lieutenant Hammond shrug off a wound to his wrist, then hit again and "killed instantly."[74] The memory of Hammond's death would be etched forever in the mind of Robert Horine: "Charley Hammond, struck three times and sinking to his knees, only to be riddled with machine gun bullets. Charley Hammond, for whom any man in 'L' Company would have given his life gladly."[75] Oliver Allard remembered, "Machine gun fire hit one of my boys and when he called for a drink of water, I crawled back slowly to offer help, but as I tipped his helmet from what I saw, it was too late."[76] Could it have been Arthur Lueskow whom Allard remembered? Or, perhaps, Albert Johnson? Maybe it was Harold Johnson. These men were all, according to "death affidavits," shot in the head by machine gun fire.[77]

Twenty-six-year-old Sergeant John Teichler, a former Menominee High football star, was ordered to the rear with a wound to his wrist. On his way back he stopped to help another soldier. According to Daley, as Teichler bent over to apply first aid he was shot in the back of the head and killed. A harassed private from Menominee, William Baker, picked off the sniper who had been firing at him, remembered Daley. "Baker laughed," Daley told the *Herald-Leader*, "and said, 'Well I got that dam [sic] dirty Hun,' and no sooner were the words uttered when he was struck directly in the forehead with a bullet that killed him."[78]

During the battle, the Michigan and Wisconsin troops could at times view one another's progress — and travails. "Advancing troops . . . on our right could be seen forging ahead," recalled Oliver Allard. "I found out later that they were the Wisconsin unit."[79] In tribute to the bravery of the Michigan men, Sheboygan, Wisconsin's Captain Paul Schmidt of the 127th Infantry observed that "These two regiments [of the 63rd Brigade] could be seen marching through a swamp and over the crest of a hill south of Sercy [sic]."[80] Schmidt continued: "Their elevation made a perfect target for the enemy guns, which poured a most deadly fire among the troops, mowing them down in fearful numbers, but they withstood the fire with great courage and marched directly into the mouth of the machine guns."[81]

Company L clawed their way up Hill 212 and, according to primary documents, fought past the western end of les Jomblets. One field message sent at 5:00 p.m. noted that Company L's battalion had "reached Les Jombles [Jomblets] Wood. . . . Later reported to have reached . . . South of Bois de la Planchette."[82] A message received at 6:25 located Company L "on the road passing the north of Bois Planchette,"[83] a placement which, if true, would have located the 3rd Battalion at the edge of the Bois Pelger, the objective for the assault stated in Field Orders No. 11.

Harry Allard wrote that "when we reached our objective, and while we lay on the ground facing the enemy with their bullets whizzing all around my body and head, I thought death would come at any moment. I had the presence of mind to offer a prayer to God, which he heard in my hour of need."[84] Allard's statement that Company L had reached their objective appears at first glance to point to an unmistakable conclusion, particularly when considered together with the field messages noted above, U.S. Army G-3 maps depicting the divisional advance, other maps such as that found in *The 32nd Division in the World War*, and even excerpts from reports written following the battle.[85] It seems from all this evidence that the 3rd Battalion of the 125th and the men of Company L had indeed crested Hill 212 and had come close to reaching the Bois Pelger.

With the possible exception of a few isolated soldiers, such an assumption would be false. The *32nd Division Summary of Operations* noted that "The 3rd Battalion, 125th Infantry . . . crossed the Ourcq River west of Moulin Caranda and attacked Les Jomblets from the southwest. The advance elements reached a line along the north Cierges — Sergy road on the brow of Cote 212."[86] These statements find their visual counterpart in the large (27"x 31 1/2") folding map from the American Battle Monuments Commission (ABMC), which delineates the front for each day of that campaign.[87]

Captain Emil Gansser remembered that "The Ourcq was crossed and the line nearly reached the crest of Hill 212, finally halting on a line facing northeast on the southern slope near the hill crest, while the enemy still occupied the top of the hill."[88] The 3rd Battalion's Robert Horine may have exaggerated, if only slightly, when he stated that "as night came on, our company consolidated the hole on *top* [my emphasis] of Hill 212 and held on through the night, raked with machine gun fire and shells."[89] Perhaps not. But clearly, the 125th Infantry's advance had stalled near the hilltop on July 31; certainly, the troops made no permanent gains beyond that point. Of course, the subsequent assaults that were required on August 1 in order to capture the areas targeted in Field Orders No. 11 are the greatest proof that Company L and the 3rd Battalion had been stymied on Hill 212.[90]

It is not particularly unusual that original G-3 maps, various primary sources, secondary sources, and secondary sources that masquerade as primary sources, should all disagree with the eventual determination of the battle lines in the ABMC material or *32nd Division: Summary of Operations.* Shortly after the war, in his "A Caution Regarding Military Documents," Theodore Calvin Pease used as one of his chief examples "the documents from which we would seek to learn the position of the front line held by a unit on a given day."[91] Pease shows how easy it is for these documents to become corrupted and how matters worsen as information moves up the chain of command:

> The platoon commander, as the original source of information, perhaps in fading daylight or early dawn, perhaps in a dense forest where no landmarks are available, possibly subject to a stinging fire if he climbs a knoll to look about him, must determine his position as best he may. This done, perhaps with a very hazy knowledge of map reading, he sends back what he guesses are the map coordinates of his position. If, as may easily happen, neither he nor his company commander has been able to look at a map for more than five minutes, he sends a rough position sketch only. . . . His company commander, battalion commander, regimental commander, each corrects the data in the light of what seems to him more authentic information.[92]

The result of all this, according to Pease, is that "a document that at first sight appears to be a source may well be a source plus a critique, the value of which depends on the skill or information of the officers who have applied

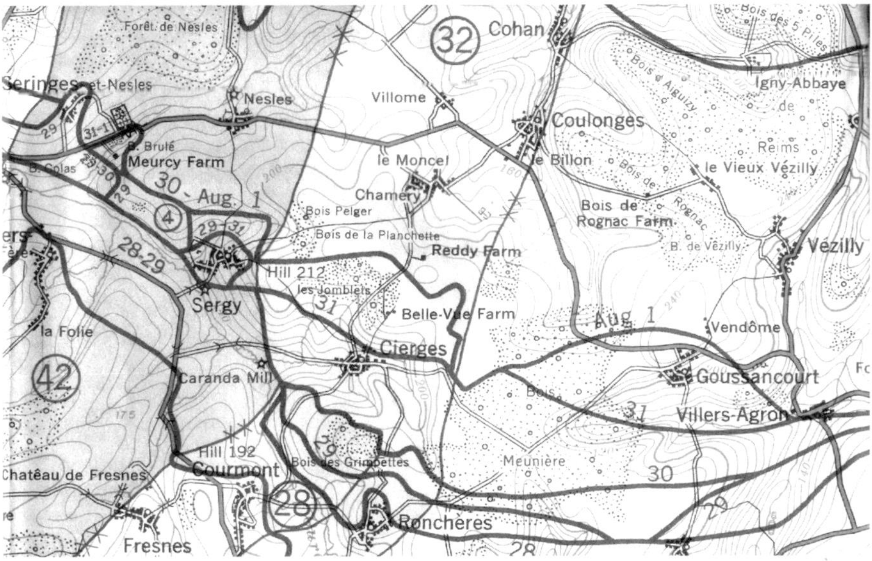

Detail from ABMC Map Showing Battle Lines July 28 to August 1, 1918.

it."[93] If the many incorrect maps are any indication, Pease might as well have been describing the depiction of the location of the 3rd Battalion of the 125th Infantry at the end of July 31. The phenomenon that Pease detailed colors histories; it makes truth difficult to discern for the reader and historian and renders some accounts of the Hill 212 battle and, of course, other events during the war, impossible to believe.

For example, according to the Joint War History Commissions' account of the day's battle, "The Michiganders dove into Les Jomblettes [Jomblets] and mopped it up, and then cleaned out the Bois Pelger. . . . It was hot work, and some wicked fighting took place before the enemy was forced to retire his line to the Bois de la Planchette, where the Americans could see another tough job in store for them."[94]

This assessment clearly fell far short of the truth. For one thing, the statement shows either an accidental or willful ignorance of the ground on which the soldiers fought or an illogical conclusion; for the Americans to "clean out the Bois Pelger" before the "enemy was forced to retire . . . to the Bois de la Planchette" would mean that the Germans were retreating forward since the Bois de la Planchette is south of the Bois Pelger. For another, there was no "mopping up" or "cleaning out" of anything on that day. *American Armies and Battlefields* put it this way: "On July 31 the 32nd Division, in an attack launched about 2:00 p.m., captured Cierges [a village near Hill 212] and Les Jomblets, but was forced by heavy hostile fire to fall back from that wood."[95] While still an evasion, that comes closer to the facts.

But the idea at stake extends beyond a mere academic argument: how far Company L or the 3rd Battalion advanced on the 31st, whether one map or another map was or is correct, just what exactly happened. The danger here is or was not just to the historian. As we can surmise, commanders make poor decisions, deadly mistakes, as a result of bad information. "Despite all protests," wrote Pease, "a unit is ordered to occupy a given trench, being assured it is vacant. It obeys orders and pays in casualties for the knowledge that the information on which the order was based was, to speak mildly, inaccurate."[96]

Entire assaults were planned based on false assumptions of the 3rd Battalion's progress on July 31. The *32nd Division Summary of Operations* commented: "*Believing* [my emphasis] that the 3d Battalion, 125th Infantry, was in Bois de la Planchette, and that the other five battalions of the brigade were along the Cierges-Sergy road [south of Bois de la Planchette], the 63d Infantry Brigade ordered an attack for 3:30 a.m., August 1, against the south and west edges of Les Jomblets and Bois Pelger."[97] At 4:30 a.m., then, a battalion of the 126th Infantry attacked les Jomblets after first "passing through the lines of the 3d Battalion, 125th Infantry, on the Cierges-Sergy road"; the 3rd Battalion was not in the Bois de la Planchette after all.[98]

The fight of July 31 was over. On August 1, the Americans and French pressed the Germans, who continued to resist fiercely. In the morning, the 2nd Battalion of the 126th Infantry briefly captured les Jomblets, Bois de la

Planchette, and the Bois Pelger. A German counterattack knocked them right back to the starting point at Hill 212.[99] That afternoon, the 32nd Division finally captured les Jomblets but was, on that day, checked from advancing farther.

In the overall scheme of the battle, however, there is something inevitable about both the confusion and mistakes made and the eventual outcome, at least in retrospect. Until August 2, every piece of ground, every wood in the area, was contested bitterly: attacks and gains were met with counterattacks and retreats. The chaos of battle reigned supreme. In essence, the Germans bought time for a withdrawal as they employed a defense in depth[100], and the two armies — one seasoned but weakening, the other naïve and inexperienced — slugged it out.

During the night of August 1-2, the Germans began an orderly retreat to strong positions on the Vesle River, some eight-nine miles from Hill 212, with the Americans in hot pursuit.[101] The 32nd Division thus attained their objectives for July 31 when the pressured Germans conceded them. The *Herald-Leader* reported accurately that the "gains" of the Americans "were made almost without resistance."[102] In sight of the Vesle, the 32nd Division was thwarted from crossing and eventually relieved. For the men of Company L, the several days of battle that had started in late July and extended through the first week of August became known as "The Drive from the Ourcq to the Vesle."

In a letter to his parents published in the *Herald-Leader* on September 9, 1918, Harry Allard wrote that "the greatest experience of my life . . . took place one afternoon in July, when the order was given to go 'over the top', and believe me from that moment on, for a stretch of eight days, it was onward through Hell."[103]

The Operation Report for July 31 from Company L's regiment noted that casualties were "Very heavy. . . . All Battalions reporting heavy losses."[104] The honor roll in *The 32nd Division in the World War* lists five officers and 149 men from the 125th Infantry as killed in action on July 31.[105] Company L's

32 enlisted men and one officer [Hammond] killed on July 31[106] were thus a highly disproportionate number of casualties, as might be expected for troops who had just assaulted a strong position. The 2nd Battalion of the 125th had suffered a bloody repulse in front of les Jomblets, but the 3rd Battalion lost 90 men killed in action, three who died of wounds, and four officers killed.[107]

Any way one looks at it, Harry Allard was right: it really was "onward through hell" for Company L of the 125th Infantry in the Red Arrow Division.

Aftermath

During World War I, many units in the American Expeditionary Forces were engaged in battles so strange and intense that it seemed as if they were waging war in complete isolation. Not only that: it often seemed to individual soldiers as if they were fighting the war single-handedly. This common theme was the experience of the 125th Infantry, 3rd Battalion, and Company L in their first assault. Robert Horine observed: "What comes back to me with the greatest force, is the feeling of being left all alone with all my buddies killed and wounded; and the failure on my part to conceive any good reason why I was not among them."[108] Lyle Cole of Company I remembered:

> Smally and I were all that was left of the eight men that started out. I asked about the others and was told they were either wounded or killed. . . . Smally and I lay there at the top of the hill, and every time we moved, bullets would scream over our heads. . . . Smally started to gripe, he only had 20 rounds of ammunition, he wanted a rifle and more ammunition. . . . I told him to go back and find a rifle and ammunition and return. If the Germans counterattacked I would need help. That was the last time I saw him. I layed there for about 3/4 of an hour. Everytime I moved, bullets would buzz around my head, too close for comfort, so I tried to be as quiet as I could.[109]

Curiously, the notion of an isolated fight for Hill 212 persists to this day. The caption on the display about Company L at the Menominee County Historical Society's Heritage Museum reads, "**COMPANY L IN WORLD WAR I CAPTURED HILL 212.**" There is no mention of the rest of the 3rd Battalion or of the regiment, brigade, or division to which Company L belonged.[110]

Three Menominee soldiers were decorated for conspicuous bravery at Hill 212, two of them posthumously. The French government awarded Oscar Falk the Croix de Guerre.[111] Today, Menominee's American Legion Post bears the name of the old captain who had yearned to command Company L in the war.

John Teichler received the Distinguished Service Cross and Croix de Guerre.[112] Teichler's citation read: "Although he was himself severely wounded in the attack on the Bois les Jamblets [sic], yet he attempted to carry in another wounded man, passing through severe machine-gun fire from the front and from the flanks. While doing so he received a second wound, which caused his death."[113] Teichler had become Company L's fallen hero of Hill 212.

Corporal Isaac Chandler of Company L survived the war and was decorated with the Croix de Guerre and Distinguished Service Cross for gallantry at Hill 212. Chandler served in the battle as a runner. "While his company was leading a battalion attack," his citation observed, "Chandler persisted in carrying messages to the battalion commander and carrying rations to the line under intensive machine-gun fire from the front and flanks, after he had been severely wounded."[114]

A fourth Menominee soldier, longtime Company L trooper Merritt "Tug" Wilson, who had gone into the July 31 battle with Oscar Falk's Company F, earned the Distinguished Service Cross and Croix de Guerre for heroism during the first week of August in the Red Arrow Division's drive to the Vesle.[115] Wilson returned to Menominee with his hearing gone in one ear and a toe half shot off; before coming home, he had comforted Lena Falk in a letter that told her of the circumstances of her husband's death.

Menominee did not learn of the Hill 212 casualties until nearly a month had passed. In fact, Oscar Falk's death was a local rumor until late-October. From the time between August 3, when the *Herald-Leader* first wrote that L was in the thick of the Aisne-Marne offensive, until August 28, when five of the nine Company L battle deaths were reported, Menominee waited in suspense for news from the local company.[116]

Predictably, that news was sobering for the townspeople of Menominee. After all, these soldiers had lived in the area and worked in the factories and offices of the once-great lumber town. According to the 1916 pre-war Company L "Muster-in Roll," Peter Boivin and John Stauber had been shoemakers; John Teichler had listed "merchant" as his occupation. Harry Allard was a draftsman and Oliver Allard, a laborer. Albert and Anton Johnson were also laborers; Harold Johnson, a box maker. Walter Pada had worked as a factory hand.[117] According to the *Herald-Leader*, before the war Arthur Lueskow had been employed at the Prescott Company, a factory that built "saw mill machinery and mine pumps."[118]

In the pre-war period, Company L had, apparently, met with some derision. After the Hill 212 fight, Menominee's Grover Thompson, who took command of Company L for good in late August, wrote to his wife, "You can tell all those people that used to knock Company L so much, that we were in one of the biggest battles of the war, and that old Co. L was sure on the job."[119]

But once the United States entered World War I, Menominee, like towns across the country, and particularly through the lens of the press, embraced the hometown company as "their boys." When Menominee soldiers from Company L were killed they became the "honored dead." And the survivors? They were "heroes all."

Still ahead for Company L were two major campaigns: the Oise-Aisne, at the end of August and into September, and the meat grinder that was the Meuse-Argonne in October. August 29 was a red-letter day for the 32nd Division: an assault at Juvigny. During the Argonne battle, the 32nd Division attacked on October 4, 5, 9, 10, 11, 14, 15, 17, and 18.[120] The division crossed the Meuse River on November 9 and attacked on November 10. On

November 11, plans to attack again were called off. At about 10:15 a.m. on November 11, forty-five minutes before World War I ended, the Chaplain of the 125th Infantry Regiment, the beloved Father William Davitt, was killed just outside the regiment's headquarters during a final artillery exchange when a shell exploded "piercing his heart."[121]

---

[1]"Company L in Terrific Battle for Eight Days," *Menominee Herald-Leader* (cited hereafter as *HL*), September 9, 1918.

[2]In an assault marked by confusion, the close similarity in the names of the two neighboring villages only made matters worse.

[3]"Machine Gun Bullet Skins Allard's Nose," *HL*, September 27, 1918.

[4]There are many sources that record the deaths of the soldiers: articles in Menominee's local daily, the *Menominee Herald-Leader*, beginning with the August 28, 1918, edition; the *Herald-Leader's* postwar compilation, *Honor Roll of Menominee County*; The Joint War History Commissions of Michigan and Wisconsin (hereafter cited as JHC), *32nd Division in the World War*; "Burial Case Files" from the National Archives; and others. A few records found in these sources — especially in *Honor Roll of Menominee County* — are at odds with others and a researcher must, therefore, exercise caution. As for Oliver Allard, he was one of only fifteen soldiers "commissioned from the ranks without being required to attend the Officer's Training Schools: These promotions were made because of extraordinary ability shown on the field of battle." Heckel, "History of the 125th," 155.

[5]The date of Albert's death was wrongly reported in some sources but records at the National Archives at College Park (hereafter cited as NACP) and elsewhere clearly establish that Albert was killed on July 31. Johnson, Albert, file folder not numbered; NM-81, E-1942, NWCH, HMFY 2000; Correspondence, Reports, Telegrams, Applications, and Other Papers Relating to Burials of Service Personnel ("Burial Case Files"), 1915-1939; Cemeterial Division; Record Group 92, Records of the Office of the Quartermaster General; NACP. Hereafter cited as "Burial Case Files"; Cemeterial Division; RG 92; NACP. Record Groups will be cited by number in this book (RG 92, for example). See Essay 3 for much more about the "Burial Case Files." The other Record Groups mentioned in this book will be RG 407, Records of the Adjutant General's Office, and RG 120, Records of the American Expeditionary Forces (World War I). As for Anton Johnson's transfer, the 128th Infantry had previously been gutted; soldiers from that unit were transferred as replacements. In April 1918, in order to rebuild the regiment, the other three regiments in the 32nd Division were required to send "every fifth man" in each company to the reconstituted 128th "to equalize the strength of the regiment and to give each rifle company less than 200 men instead of the usual strength of 250 enlisted men." Heckel, "History of the 125th," 16. Donnelly, "History of Company 'G'," Chapter V, had it that every third man went to the 128th.

[6]Or, as it was put in *Infantry in Battle*: "A unit . . . must not be permitted to drift aimlessly into battle." This happened time after time in the American Expeditionary Forces (AEF) in World War I. Lanham, *Infantry in Battle*, 138. Lanham, 138-143, influenced my thought on the Hill 212 battle in general.

[7]See notes 13 and 15 below.

[8]Bruce, *Fraternity of Arms*, 250. Historian Robert Bruce devotes an entire chapter in *Fraternity of Arms* to the Aisne-Marne offensive. Bruce states flatly: "The Second Battle of the Marne was the turning point of World War I." He calls the summer of 1918 "the critical moment of the 1918 campaign, and indeed of the Great War Itself." Later, Bruce asserts that "Although British historians

laud the accomplishments of [Douglas] Haig's offensive at Amiens on 8 August as the moment when Germany's leaders realized they were beaten, the Franco-American victory at the Second Battle of the Marne was the real turning point." Bruce, *Fraternity of Arms*, 219; 246. But see also, for example, Tim Travers, who writes that "If a turning point can be found in 1918, it was the French counteroffensive at the Marne, followed by the Amiens offensive." To Travers, these and later "allied victories" in 1918 were manifestations of three factors: "the cumulative effects of attrition on the German Army"; "overwhelming allied superiority in technology and material"; and the allies' having "perfected the art of combined-arms warfare." "The Allied Victories, 1918," 288-289.

[9]Keegan, *First World War*, 407. Bruce, in *Fraternity of Arms*, 204, estimated the distance as fifty miles.

[10]Travers, "The Allied Victories, 1918," 279. Travers puts well the assessment of many historians: "It was the anticipation of this steady accumulation of AEF troops that forced the German army into their ultimately ill-fated spring offensives. The arrival of the AEF produced an enormous psychological boost for the allies and ensured an eventual allied victory, even if the raw and inexperienced performance of the AEF in the field was understandably flawed at times." "The Allied Victories, 1918," 284. See also Bruce, *Fraternity of Arms*, 220; Bruce writes that during July 1918, "313,410" American troops arrived in France. According to John Keegan, Ludendorff "attributed the growing malaise in his army and the sense of 'looming defeat' that afflicted it to 'the sheer number of Americans arriving daily at the front.'" Keegan, *First World War*, 411.

[11]American Battle Monuments Commission (hereafter cited as ABMC), *32nd Division: Summary of Operations, 8.*

[12]Bullard, *Personalities and Reminiscences*, 226.

[13]JHC, *32nd Division in the World War*, 70.

[14]Estimates of AEF soldiers who died during the war (killed in action or from disease or illness) differ. Niall Ferguson, for example, gives 114,000 (based on several sources) as the figure for American war dead in his *Pity of War*, 295; Robert Bruce states that American deaths were "approximately 126,000" in *Fraternity of Arms*, 288. Bruce uses the term "killed," which is inaccurate, but this figure is commonly given for overall deaths. The number of AEF soldiers who died from disease more than doubled the number killed in action, but not in the 125th Infantry Regiment, according to Heckel, "History of the 125th," 98: "The ratio of battle deaths to disease deaths in the 125th Infantry was 60 to 1."

[15]Trask, "The Entry of the USA Into the War and its Effects," 252. Of course, Bruce, for example, would go further than this in praise of the AEF. The 63rd Brigade Commander, General William Conner, was relieved of command on August 5, 1918, during the "Drive from the Ourcq to the Vesle," before the 32nd was relieved on August 6-7. At one juncture on August 3, according to the terse *32nd Division: Summary of Operations*, the 63rd "did not attack"—apparently, when ordered to do so. ABMC, *32nd Division: Summary of Operations*, 19. Much of the soon-to-be-relieved Conner's report to Division Commander William Haan on August 3 reads like an apologia: liaison could not be established on the right or left flanks, troops were exhausted, and so forth. Wrote Conner: "When I finally discovered that I was so far ahead of troops on my flank and in case I advanced there would be no corresponding movement on my right, I therefore decided it would be useless to cross the VESLE until it could be done by concerted movement and I decided to maintain the position which the troops are now occupying." 63rd Brigade Commander [Conner] to 32nd Division Commander [Haan], August 3, 1918; 63 Inf Brig Operation Reports, 1918, file folder 33.6; 32nd Division, Historical 64.4-66.3, 63rd Infantry Brigade; World War I Organization Records; RG 120; NACP. Bullard speaks of disagreements with the French that led to "the loss of his brigade by an American Brigadier" during the Aisne-Marne battle: "The brigade apparently became stubborn and the orders were ill, or not at all executed." Bullard, *Personalities and Reminiscences*, 227. Despite the 63rd's failure to attack on August 3, the "recalcitrant" brigade does

not appear to have been the 63rd. General Robert Alexander, who replaced Conner, noted that he received his orders on August 1 (unbeknownst to either General William Haan, the 32nd Division's commander, or to Conner), and Haan, at least, was well-satisfied with Conner. In fact, the surprised Haan made Alexander's arrival at the 32nd relatively unpleasant. Alexander, *Memories of the World War*, 65-67; 73. In any event, all this is something of a counterpoint to the all-conquering theme that pervades some accounts of the "Drive from the Ourcq to the Vesle."

[16]Center of Military History, United States Army (hereafter cited as CMH), *Order of Battle*, 179. Evidence that some Company L troops wore their National Guard collar insignia comes from the "Burial Case Files" in RG 92 at NACP.

[17]Half of Company L was transferred to Company K when the 125th was formed and half of Company C joined L. Heckel, "History of the 125th," 9. Also, more soldiers were transferred from L to help round out the 128th Infantry, as mentioned in note 5 above.

[18]For example, Oliver Allard surmised that "Some 57 [Company L] soldiers from Menominee and other parts of Menominee County steeled themselves as they waited the command to start their drive against the German army who were holding Hill 212." Allard, "Sixty Years Ago," 3. Erstwhile Company L commander, and Commander of Company F, 125th Infantry, Oscar Falk, wrote: "I have Tug [Wilson] with me and he is the only one from Co. L. The rest of the company is all split up and mixed with other companies." This exaggeration contained an element of truth. Oscar Falk to "Grand Ma," May 25, 1918, The Menominee County Historical Society Michael J. Anuta Research Center (hereafter cited as MCHS-ARC). The figure of 200-215 represents a broad (but accurate, in my view) guess based on my knowledge of the size of companies at the time and on strength returns from the 125th Infantry and for Company L; returns are missing for the end of July (!) but could be found for Company L in June (206 men and officers present) and for the regiment in August (including a figure for Company L). See Strength Return, Company L, 125th Infantry, June 1918; 125th Infantry Companies, file folder not numbered; Infantry Regiments,123 (Companies)-125; World War I Strength Returns; RG 407; NACP. Also, see Strength Return, 125th Infantry, August, 1918; 125th Infantry 1917-1918, file folder not numbered; Infantry Regiments, 123 (Companies)-125; World War I Strength Returns; RG 407; NACP.

[19]"Cable Tells of Wounds Received by Capt. Falk," *HL*, September 5, 1918.

[20]Donnelly, "History of Company 'G'," Chapter VI.

[21]"Final Rites of Oscar Falk Tomorrow P.M.," *HL*, Sept. 3, 1921. Note the date of this newspaper article and how long it took for Falk's body to be returned home for (re)burial.

[22]Merritt Wilson to Lena (Mrs. Oscar) Falk, December 29, 1918, MCHS-ARC.

[23]R. M. Cooley to Lena (Mrs. Oscar) Falk, April 3, 1920, MCHS-ARC.

[24]Ibid.

[25]"Capt. Oscar Falk Died of Wounds on August 1st," *HL*, October 23, 1918. Note how long it took for Lena Falk to receive definite word of her husband's death.

[26]Allard, "Sixty Years Ago," 2.

[27]ABMC, *32nd Division: Summary of Operations*, 11.

[28]Ibid.

[29]Cole, "1918 Diary," 36.

[30]Donnelly, "History of Company 'G'," Chapter VI.

[31]US Army, "Report on Operations," "Phase I," 3.

[32]Consolidated Operations Report, August 14, 1918; 63 Inf Brig Operation Reports, 1918, file folder 33.6; 32nd Division, Historical 64.4-66.3, 63rd Infantry Brigade; World War I Organization Records; RG 120; NACP.

[33]JHC, *32nd Division in the World War*, 58.

[34]Schmidt, *Co. C*, 37.

[35]United States Army, "Report on Operations," "Phase 1," 9.

[36]Ibid.

[37]United States Army, "Report on Operations," "Phase 1," 3.

[38]The order in which the battalions of the 63rd Brigade attacked is clearly delineated in ABMC, *32nd Division: Summary of Operations*, 12. The 3rd Battalion of the 125th Infantry led the attack on the left (west) and the 2nd Battalion on the right (east). Emil Gansser noted the movements that the 2nd Battalion had to make in order to attack: "On the right, the attacking troops moved east and crossed the Ourcq River. . . . The right battalion moved through the northern half of Grimpettes Woods, and when the left battalion reached the top of the hill northwest of these woods, the direction of advance was changed to north, and its left became a pivot on which the line swung to the left, and the attack continued north toward the village of Cierges." The point here is that the 2nd Battalion had to march east first in order to make a frontal attack on Cierges and les Jomblets; they had not encamped the previous evening with the 127th Infantry directly to their right. Gansser, *History of the 126th*, 102. Mathews appears in Roster of Officers: Field and Staff, Headquarters, 125th Infantry, July 31, 1918; 125th Infantry Rosters, 1918-1919, file folder not numbered; Infantry Regiments, 123 (Companies)-125; World War I Strength Returns; RG 407; NACP. According to Heckel, "History of the 125th," 31, "Major Mathews was relieved of command of the 3rd Battalion on August 16th." One factor that might have influenced the 125th's deployment and assault on July 31 was the wounding of the 1st Battalion Commander, Major Augustus Gansser, on July 30. An account of this incident is found in Heckel, "History of the 125th," 27.

[39]Douglas MacArthur was the 42nd Division's Chief of Staff at this time. On August 6 he was placed in command of the 42nd's 84th Infantry Brigade. CMH, *Order of Battle*, 272. Naturally, he was stylish and often-photographed — even then (see photograph in Persico, *Eleventh Month*). Sergeant Joyce Kilmer, who served in that division, had been killed on the Ourcq the day before (July 30). An account of his death appears in Persico, *Eleventh Month*, 260. Kilmer is buried in the Oise-Aisne American Cemetery at Fere-en-Tardenois, as are 6,000 other soldiers, including Menominee's Albert and Anton Johnson. ABMC, *American Armies*, 76; 462. The Johnson brothers' records are filed alphabetically in the "Burial Case Files"; Cemeterial Division; RG 92; NACP.

[40]Allard, "Sixty Years Ago," 3.

[41]JHC, *32nd Division in the World War*, 59.

[42]Ibid.

[43]Gansser, *History of the 126th*, 109; CMH, *United States Army*, 381; 664; 673- 674. Allard, "Sixty Years Ago," 4. Allard wrote that Company L faced elements of three divisions during the Aisne-Marne offensive: the 200th, 216th, and the 4th Prussian Guard. A map entitled "Combined Order of Battle of the French Fifth and Sixth Armies and German Seventh Army in the Aisne-Marne, 30 July 1918," shows that this is probably true; the map places the 216th and 200th from west to east on the front of the 32nd on July 30 with the 4th Guard Division to the west of the 216th. CMH, *United States Army*, 381.

[44]Field Orders No. 11, July 31, 1918; 63rd Inf Brig Field Orders-1918, file folder 32.1; 32nd Division, Historical 64.4-66.3, 63rd Infantry Brigade; World War I Organization Records; RG 120; NACP.

[45]ABMC, *32nd Division: Summary of Operations*, 12.

[46]"42 Company L Boys Killed in Five Hours," *HL*, February 5, 1919.

[47]Cole, "1918 Diary," 37.

[48]Donnelly, "History of Company 'G'," Chapter VI.

[49]Gansser, *History of the 126th*, 102.

[50]Summary of Reports Received and Sent at P.C., 63rd Infantry Brigade, July 31, 1918, Commanding Officer 2nd Bn. [Wilson] to Commanding Officer 125th Inf. [Morrow], 5; 63 Inf

Brig Field Messages, file folder 32.16; 32nd Division, Historical 64.4-66.3, 63rd Infantry Brigade; World War I Organization Records; RG 120; NACP. I could find no battalion attack orders for the 2nd or 3rd Battalions, 125th Infantry, in the record and, given the circumstances, it would not surprise me if no written orders were issued at that level. One can only hope that the battalion orders given contained more specific directions than the 63rd Brigade Orders (Field Orders No. 11), which, for the 3rd Battalion, amounted to: advance until you reach the Bois Pelger and we will support you with artillery fire. See Lanham, *Infantry in Battle*, 139-143, for a hauntingly similar example.

[51]Allard, "Sixty Years Ago," 3.

[52]Cole, "1918 Diary," 37. Accounts differ even on the size of the Ourcq River. Emil Gansser wrote that "in the vicinity of Cierges and Sergy it [the Ourcq] is not over eight feet wide, with steep banks." Gansser, *History of the 126th*, 100-101.

[53]Allard, "Sixty Years Ago," 3-4.

[54]"42 Co. L Boys Killed in Five Hours," *HL*, February 5, 1919.

[55]Here I will emphasize a point made earlier in the text: according to the field order, the assault was to be made by the 3rd and 2nd Battalions of the 125th Infantry Regiment; the 1st Battalion of the 125th was to "maintain its present position until our first and second lines have passed when it will form as a third line battalion in rear of our right." This wording quite possibly had something to do with the confusion that ensued in the July 31 battle, especially given the late issuance and arrival of the orders. Field Orders No. 11, July 31, 1918; 63rd Inf Brig Field Orders-1918, file folder 32.1; 32nd Division, Historical 64.4-66.3, 63rd Infantry Brigade; World War I Organization Records; RG 120; NACP. The type of tactics employed during the attack on Hill 212 are critiqued in Nenninger, "Tactical Dysfunction in the AEF," 178: "Rigid plans of attack, lines of infantry advancing over open ground without regard for concealment or cover, little use of fire and maneuver, and improper employment of infantry supporting arms, were typical of American infantry in the offenses of the Summer and Fall of 1918." At least some of the problems the 125th Infantry and Company L experienced at Hill 212 appear to have had their genesis in Field Orders No. 11.

[56]Emil Gansser wrote: "In the left brigade sector, the 3rd Battalion, 125th Infantry, made the attack. . . . At the jump off the attacking battalion was in line on the northern slope of the hill just east of the La Mott farm. The direction of attack was northeast and the objective was Hill 212." Gansser, *History of the 126th*, 103. Note that the objective is listed as Hill 212 instead of that stated in Field Orders No. 11: the Bois Pelger, a more difficult objective to attain.

[57]See for example, Summary of Reports Received and Sent at P.C., 63rd Infantry Brigade, July 31, 1918, Commanding Officer 126th Infantry [Westnedge] to Commanding General, 63rd Infantry Brigade [Connor], 3; 63 Inf Brig Field Messages, file folder 32.16; 32nd Division, Historical 64.4-66.3, 63rd Infantry Brigade; World War I Organization Records; RG 120; NACP. Field Orders No. 11 said nothing about Company L and the rest of the 3rd Battalion, 125th Infantry, passing through lines of American troops on the left of the 63rd Brigade's line. Had the order done so, this would have been a possible explanation for the battalion's expectation of seeing other American troops. One can then only assume that the orders were not understood or poorly executed, or that information is incomplete (or that my understanding of extant information is incomplete). Additional written communications that might make the issue of the misunderstood orders clear appear to no longer exist; in any event, I was unable to find them. Of course, verbally relayed messages can be misunderstood easily. It seems unlikely that the battalion leading the attack could have expected to see friendly troops in the direction of the attack if they were not to pass through those troops first. The field messages might be referring to the possibility of the 3rd Battalion's seeing 42nd Division troops to the west of the 63rd Brigade; given the accounts of the soldiers involved, this is unlikely. The combination of the 2nd Battalion moving to the right in

order to attack les Jomblets frontally and the 1st Battalion's maneuvering to the rear to form a reserve as per Field Orders No. 11 apparently allowed at least the bulk of the 3rd Battalion to advance without coming into contact with other friendly units. On the other hand, the 3rd Battalion's Robert Horine remembered moving "through what remained of the Rainbow Division on the Ourcq"; if, as I believe, Horine was with Company M, this would have placed M on the far left of the battalion during the assault. Heckel, "History of the 125th," 116.

58Cole, "1918 Diary," 37.

59"42 Co. L Boys Killed in Five Hours," *HL*, February 5, 1919. The comment from *Infantry in Battle* bears repeating: "A unit must be engaged in accordance with a definite plan. It must not be permitted to drift aimlessly into battle." Lanham, *Infantry in Battle*, 138. Confusion also reigned supreme with the 2nd Battalion, as noted in the text above. Major Guy Wilson complained that during the assault there had been "No adequate telephone service. No adequate artillery preparation." Summary of Reports Received and Sent at P.C., 63rd Infantry Brigade, July 31, 1918, Commanding Officer 2nd Bn. [Wilson] to Commanding Officer 125th Inf. [Morrow], 5; 63 Inf Brig Field Messages, file folder 32.16; 32nd Division, Historical 64.4-66.3, 63rd Infantry Brigade; World War I Organization Records; RG 120; NACP. Captain Emil Gansser remembered that "the attack was made without artillery preparation." Gansser, *History of the 126th*, 102. This may or may not have been true, but there was neither coordination between units nor sufficient artillery support for the attack on Hill 212. Daley's statement that "no battle raged" is also testimony to the lack of coordination between the artillery and infantry branches during the assault.

60"42 Co. L Boys Killed in Five Hours," *HL*, February 5, 1919.

61Ibid.

62"Jos. M. Stauber, Menominee Hero, Came Home Today," *HL*, January 31, 1919.

63Ibid. Or was it? Stauber's war wounds apparently contributed mightily to his early death from tuberculosis just a few years later. "Wounded at Chateau Thierry, Dies at Denver: Joe Stauber of Menominee's Own Co. L, Never Regained His Health," *HL*, November 10, 1923; State of Michigan, "Registrar's Permit for Burial or Removal," November 9, 1923, Riverside Cemetery, Menominee, Michigan.

64"42 Co. L Boys Killed in Five Hours," *HL*, February 5, 1919.

65Summary of Reports Received and Sent at P.C., 63rd Infantry Brigade, July 31, 1918, Brigade Liaison Officer at Flint to Commanding General, 63rd Infantry Brigade [Conner], 3; 63 Inf Brig Field Messages, file folder 32.16; 32nd Division, Historical 64.4-66.3, 63rd Infantry Brigade; World War I Organization Records; RG 120; NACP.

66"42 Co. L Boys Killed in Five Hours," *HL*, February 5, 1919.

67Allard, "Sixty Years Ago," 4. The operative word here is "awhile." Just what "awhile" means is explored later in this chapter.

68Summary of Reports Received and Sent at P.C., 63rd Infantry Brigade, July 31, 1918, Brig L.O. at Flint, Byran to 63d Lo. O. Lt. Harcourt, Harcourt at Fresne, 2; 63 Inf Brig Field Messages, file folder 32.16; 32nd Division, Historical 64.4-66.3, 63rd Infantry Brigade; World War I Organization Records; RG 120; NACP.

69"42 Co. L Boys Killed in Five Hours," *HL*, February 5, 1919. An interesting rumination on the vagaries of surrender can be found in Ferguson, *Pity of War*, Chapter 13, "The Captor's Dilemma." Daley exaggerated these casualty figures; 32 men and one officer from Company L died at Hill 212, as noted later in the text of this essay. Figures for those wounded remain hard to determine at the company level. The August 1918 Strength Return for the 125th Infantry listed Company L's "Strength Last Monthly Return" — presumably numbers taken from the July 1918 Strength Return — as 126 men and four officers. These monthly reports purported to show the "Condition of the Command at Midnight" on the last day of the month in question. If these figures are accurate, Company L lost at least 70 men killed and wounded — given my earlier estimate of 200-215 Company L soldiers who fought at Hill 212. Further, it appears, then, that *at least* 37 men were wounded badly enough to be listed. Strength Return, 125th Infantry, August 1918; 125th Infantry 1917-1918, file folder not numbered; Infantry Regiments, 123 (Companies)-125; World War I Strength Returns; RG 407; NACP.

[70]Heckel, "History of the 125th," 116. See also, Nenninger, "Tactical Dysfunction in the AEF," 178. Timothy Nenninger writes on the American attack at Soissons earlier in July: "The Americans had advanced in steady lines across open wheat fields as German machine-gunners shot them down." The scene repeated itself in the assault of July 31.

[71]Gansser, *History of the 126th*, 103. It appears, then, that the 3rd Battalion received enfilade fire. Gansser, among others, wrote (in the page cited) that "The enemy had placed a large Red Cross flag in the steeple of the church in Cierges . . . it was discovered that enemy snipers were located in the church steeple." After Lyle Cole was wounded, he told the medic attending to him that "I couldn't understand the bullet came from in back of me and toward Ciergies. He informed me that they came from the church tower in Ciergies, that two Germans had a machine gun and a good commanding view of Hill #212 and 'I' Company, and had killed or wounded so many of our boys." Cole, "1918 Diary," 39.

[72]Heckel, "History of the 125th," 116.

[73]"42 Co. L Boys Killed in Five Hours," *HL*, February 5, 1919.

[74]Ibid.

[75]Heckel, "History of the 125th," 117. Horine's section of the regiment's history was entitled "A Platoon Leader's Impressions of the Ourcq-Vesle Drive of the 32nd Division." My unproven impression from Horine's discussion is that he was a soldier in M Company. Did he really see Company L's Hammond fall? It certainly seems as if he did.

[76]Allard, "Sixty Years Ago," 4.

[77]"Death affidavits" for each of these soldiers appear in their "Burial Case Files"; Cemeterial Division; RG 92; NACP.

[78]"42 Co. L Boys Killed in Five Hours," *HL*, February 5, 1919. Teichler's death and its aftermath is discussed in Essay 3 of this book.

[79]Allard, "60 Years Ago," 4.

[80]Schmidt, *Co. C*, 41.

[81]Ibid.

[82]Summary of Reports Received and Sent at P.C., 63rd Infantry Brigade, July 31, 1918, Commanding Officer 126th Infantry [Westnedge] to Commanding General, 63rd Infantry Brigade [Connor], 3; 63 Inf Brig Field Messages, file folder 32.16; 32nd Division, Historical 64.4-66.3, 63rd Infantry Brigade; World War I Organization Records; RG 120, NACP

[83]Summary of Reports Received and Sent at P.C., 63rd Infantry Brigade, July 31, 1918, Commanding Officer 126th Infantry [Westnedge] to Commanding General, 63rd Infantry Brigade [Connor], 5; 63 Inf Brig Field Messages, file folder 32.16; 32nd Division, Historical 64.4-66.3, 63rd Infantry Brigade; World War I Organization Records; RG 120, NACP.

[84]"Company L in Terrific Battle for Eight Days," *HL*, September 9, 1918. There may have been confusion, also, about the objective of the assault. No less an authority than Captain Emil Gansser wrote that the "plan of attack was to cross the Ourcq River and take Hill 212, the village of Cierges, and Jomblets Woods." Gansser, *History of the 126th*, 102. All this was indeed part of the plan but was not the assault's stated objective. The initial French orders (from the 38th Corps) for an assault on July 31 had as one of its primary objectives the taking of Hill 212. In the "Report on Operations of the Thirty-Second Division" for the Aisne-Marne campaign, Major-General Haan wrote: "In compliance with a request from the Corps Commander that an attempt be made to capture the village of Cierges and Hill 212 on the left part of the sector, an attack was prepared and launched on July 31st. *My plan was to carry the line further forward to include the strong position extending*

across the sector from Hill 230 on the right, including BELLEVUE FARM and small woods on the left (BOIS-de-la-PLANCHETTE) [my emphasis]." The French plan, in hindsight, seems to have been more reasonable. General Conner, acting under Haan's instructions, actually went even further in Field Orders No.11 than Haan implies here; Conner's orders state: "Its [the 63rd Brigade's] objective will be the BOIS PELGER and the BOIS du PALGER [sic]." The differences are notable between the assault objective from Field Orders No. 11, the objective as stated in "Report on Operations," and both the initial French objective and the remembered goal—Hill 212. US Army, "Report on Operations," "Phase 1," 3. Field Orders No. 11, July 31, 1918; 63rd Inf Brig Field Orders-1918, file folder 32.1; 32nd Division, Historical 64.4-66.3, 63rd Infantry Brigade; World War I Organization Records; RG 120; NACP.

[85]Map Showing Daily Advance of the 32nd. Division, Aisne-Marne Offensive, 29th. July to 6th Aug. '18; 32nd Division Map #1, file folder not numbered; 32nd Division Folders 4-9, Index 32nd Div. Maps, Folders 1-10; A.E.F General Headquarters G-3 Reports; RG 120; NACP. G-3 (or, today, G3) refers to "operations and training." The JHC map is similar (albeit without the hand-coloring); *32nd Division in the World War*, 56. Another G-3 map is even more blatantly wrong than these two maps: Advance of the 32nd Division, July 29th to Aug. 5, 1918; Folder 7; 32nd Division Folders 4-9, Index 32nd Div. Maps, Folders 1-10; A.E.F General Headquarters G-3 Reports; RG 120; NACP. These maps also show the 2nd Battalion advancing farther than they did on July 31. The maps do not reflect what credible sources demonstrate: that the lead elements in the 2nd Battalion's attack were beaten in front of les Jomblets and driven back. To switch the focus from the 3rd Battalion to the 2nd for a moment is helpful in ascertaining the accuracy of the G-3 maps and others. See "Maps" in Plates section, 95-97 in this book.

[86]ABMC, *32nd Division: Summary of Operations*, 12.

[87]ABMC, *American Armies*, "American Operations in the Aisne-Marne Region, May 31-October 12, 1918"; detached map in rear pocket of book.

[88]Gansser, *History of the 126th*, 103.

[89]Heckel, "History of the 125th," 116. Company I's Lyle Cole also wrote: "When we reached the top of the hill orders were given to lay down." Cole, "A 1918 Diary," 37-38.

[90]The battle for the woods and hills in the Sergy-Cierges area was still a fierce one on August 1. The German plan was to hold off the advance of the French 6th Army until the evening of August 1-2. On another note, all this is not to say that isolated pockets of men failed to advance past the main line on July 31. In fact, platoon leader Robert Horine — probably in Company M — remembered "Big 'Mike' Udell, who fought the war in his own way": his "squad went farther forward that afternoon than any element in the Regiment; to this fact, the graves of the entire squad across the road are mute evidence." Heckel, "History of the 125th," 117. Note that information about soldiers killed in battle is easier to trace than for those who survived; thus, I do not know that Horine was in Company M, although this is a virtual certainty. I do know that Corporal Michael Udell was with Company M: he is listed in the honor roll in JHC, *32nd Division in the World War*, 288.

[91]Pease, "A Caution Regarding Military Documents," 282.

[92]Ibid.

[93]Ibid., 283. This is, of course, assuming that there is an interest in records at all. In the preface to his memoir on World War I, General Robert Lee Bullard fairly chortled: "Records! I had no time to gather them." Bullard, *Personalities and Reminiscences*.

[94]JHC, *32nd Division in the World War*, 59-60.

[95]ABMC, *American Armies*, 69.

[96]Pease, "A Caution Regarding Military Documents," 283.

[97]ABMC, *32nd Division: Summary of Operations*, 13.

[98]Ibid., 14.

[99]Ibid.

[100]This tactic of successive tiers of defense developed as the war dragged on. Referring to the action of July 29, a German operations report noted that "the enemy attacks were checked everywhere partly in our front line, partly in the defense zone organized in depth." CMH, *United States Army in the World War, Vol. 5*, 673. A good explanation of defense in depth, which the French employed during the German assault of July 15 and just prior to the counterattack of July 18, can be found in Bruce, *Fraternity of Arms*, 229-230.

[101]The German Army had planned the August 1-2 retreat to the Vesle since July 27, according to a German operation report: "It was at this point that the time was set for continuing the withdrawal in the night of August 1-2. The designation of this time was based on a definite calculation: it was to afford the opportunity to move all material south of the VESLE back across the river." CMH, *United States Army*, 673.

[102]"Huns Withdraw in Defense and Yanks Sweep On," HL, August 2, 1918.

[103]"Company L in Terrific Battle for Eight Days," *HL*, September 9, 1918.

[104]Operation Report, 125th Infantry, 0 to 24, July 31st, 1918; 125th. Inf Daily Operation Reports, 33.1; 64th Infantry Brigade, 125th Infantry Regiment; 32nd Division, Historical; World War I Organization Records; RG 120; NACP.

[105]JHC, *32nd Division in the World War*, 217-294.

[106]Ibid. One unit in the 3rd Battalion, Company M, suffered more men killed than Company L, possibly because of Udell's rush ahead of the line (see note 90). M Company lost one officer and 37 enlisted men killed in action and one additional soldier who died of wounds. Together, Companies L and M lost 69 of the 149 enlisted men from the 125th Infantry regiment who were killed in action on July 31. The figure of 149 killed is corroborated in the Organizational List of the Members of the American Expeditionary Forces Who Died in Service Abroad During the World War, Organizations with 32nd Army Division, November 6, 1920; Casualties, 32nd Division, file folder not numbered; Office File, Casualties of the AEF By Division, 1-36 Division; World War I Organization Records; RG 407; NACP. Two soldiers were listed here as dying on July 21; I found this possible but unlikely, and thus split the difference when I counted. The resulting figure, 149, matched the number of enlisted men killed according to figures derived from the JHC account. Of course, the exact number is not what matters, but this is a good ballpark figure. As for soldiers wounded in action, between July 30 and August 1, the 125th Infantry suffered 419 wounded, and more than 200 additional soldiers of the 125th were wounded during the remainder of the "Drive from the Ourcq to the Vesle." The Division as a whole sustained 3,847 casualties between July 27 and August 11. ABMC, *32nd Division: Summary of Operations*, 22.

[107]JHC, 32nd Division in the World War, 217-294.

[108]Heckel, "History of the125th," 117.

[109]Cole, "A 1918 Diary," 38.

[110]These were initial errors of emphasis or of context (in my view), but understandable. Another questionable formulation is the use in the display of the word "captured," which is a trifle optimistic but, in general, the original display, finished in 1981, was conservative or preservationist in nature. It conserved a finite number of items and the memory of Company L. More about the museum display appears in this book's Afterword. Please read note 4 in the Afterword for a gloss on the sort of mistakes that are much more destructive to social memory. For information on the original display, see Flo McDermott, "Co. L Comes to Life in Historical Museum Exhibit," Around Town, *HL*, July 16, 1981.

[111]Landrum, *Michigan in the World War*, 133.

[112]Ibid., 65; 218-219.

[113]Ibid., 65.

[114]Ibid., 26, 115.

[115]Ibid., 71, 232. Merritt Wilson was the genuine article. He was a tower of strength to the men from Company G. On the way to the Vesle, F and G Companies were combined because F had lost so many men on July 31. Donnelly, "History of Company 'G'," Chapter VI.

[116]See "Five Members of Co. L, Menominee, Die Fighting for Liberty's Cause," *HL*, August 28, 1918.

[117]Muster-in Roll of Company L of the 33rd Infantry Regiment, Michigan National Guard, July 8, 1916, MCHS-ARC.

[118]The Prescott Company is described in Senior English Class of 1925, "History of Menominee, 1910-1925," MCHS-ARC. "Memorial Rites to be Said for 3 Co. L Heroes," *HL*, August 30, 1918.

[119]"Lieutenant Thompson Now in Command of Company 'L'," *HL*, September 11, 1918.

[120]For brief synopses of the action, see ABMC, *32nd Division: Summary of Operations*, 24; 36-37. Four officers from the 125th alone were killed on August 29 according to Heckel, "History of the 125th," 152. Captain Joseph Donnelly of Company G, 125th Infantry, was seriously wounded on October 9 in the Argonne. On that day, two fresh-faced lieutenants reported to Donnelly. "Within an hour both of these young Lieutenants were dead and he [Donnelly] never did get their correct names."; "History of Company 'G'," Chapter VIII. It is possible that his wounding on this date saved Donnelly. On October 10, five officers of the 125th were killed in action or died of wounds according to Heckel, "History of the 125th," 152.

[121]A detailed account of Davitt's death appears in Heckel, "History of the 125th," 69-70. Davitt's virtues are also extolled in this source on page 132. His photograph appears in JHC, *The 32nd Division in the World War*, 277.

Essay 2

Patriotism, Propaganda, and Whistling in the Dark

During World War I, on June 17, 1918, Menominee, Michigan, staged a full-scale German book burning.

This was the biggest story in the campaign to whip the minds of area citizens into war fever — a curious mixture of hatred and fear — while Company L of Menominee fought real, not illusory, battles in France. Business leaders in Menominee's American Club organized the spectacle. The American Club was the wartime name of the former Commercial Club and the forerunner of the post-war Chamber of Commerce.[1]

Plans for the burning included hiring Bergfor's band (note the German name), organizing a parade, singing patriotic songs, tarring books. No detail was too small for the watchful eye of the American Club. "Moving pictures may be taken of the burning of the books," announced the *Menominee Herald-Leader*.[2]

1918 home movies of a book burning? Move over, Zapruder. Where is the archive when we need it?

Right here, that is where. The movies — if they were ever taken — are long gone. But photographs of the book burning are housed at the Menominee County Historical Society's Michael J. Anuta Research Center, and the event is documented in the annals of the *Herald-Leader* at the Research Center and on microfilm at Spies Public Library.

Most of the books that were burned were textbooks from Menominee High School. These were deemed "EVIL PROPAGANDA." Also, the denizens of Menominee and Marinette were invited to add their contribution to the blaze: "any German books, phonograph records, music or pictures, and anything 'Made in Germany'."[3]

Spies Public Library did not participate. On June 11, at a "special meeting of the board of directors of the AMERICAN CLUB," John J. O'Hara, American Club President, "brought up the matter of burning the German books in the Spies public library. This matter was referred to committee."[4] Longtime Menominee business leader Augustus Spies, donor of the library, had died in 1915. According to his obituary, Spies was born in Hesse, Darmstadt, Germany in 1836 and had arrived in the United States when he was fourteen.[5] O'Hara had to get his books elsewhere.

The June 18 *Herald-Leader* proclaimed, "Great Throng Rejoices As Books Burn: Biggest Crowd Ever Assembled in Menominee for Any Patriotic Occasion Shouts, Sings and Yells as German Kultur Goes Up in Smoke." The crowd was estimated at 6,000 to 8,000. "Preceding the program at the High school campus," the article continued, "the scene of the burning out of the German Language in Menominee, a parade over a half mile in length, in which hundreds took part, marched from the business district to the school grounds."[6]

O'Hara gave a speech at the event that was printed in full in the *Herald-Leader* under the headline, "Address at Book Burning Made Tremendous Hit." "We have allowed our schools and institutions of learning to become saturated with German kultur by teaching German and employing German agents as professors," O'Hara intoned, "but thank Almighty God today the American people have unmasked German kultur and delivered it into the hands of the devil for the archives of hell."[7]

Here O'Hara and his throng of supporters have done us the favor of introducing two concepts. First, that of the destruction of archives or the archive.[8] French philosopher Jacques Derrida knew whereof he spoke when he wrote about "a decisive paradox" inherent in the archive:

> If there is no archive without consignation in an *external place* which assures the possibility of memorization, of repetition, of reproduction, or of reimpression, then we must also remember that repetition itself, the logic of repetition, indeed the repetition

> compulsion, remains, according to Freud, indissociable with the death drive. And thus from destruction. Consequence: right on that which permits and conditions archivization, we will never find anything other than that which exposes to destruction, and in truth menaces with destruction, introducing, a priori, forgetfulness and the archiviolithic into the heart of the monument. Into the "by heart" itself. The archive always works, and a priori, against itself.[9]

Second, O'Hara introduces the idea of the archives of hell. Or ARCHIVES OF HELL. Derrida would have positively licked his chops:

> The model . . . also incorporates what may seem, in the form of a destruction drive, to contradict even the conservation drive, what we would call here the archive drive. It is what I called earlier, and in view of this internal contradiction, archive fever. There would indeed be no archive desire without the radical finitude, without the possibility of forgetfulness which does not limit itself to repression. Above all, and this is the most serious, beyond or within this simple limit called finiteness or finitude, there is no archive fever without the threat of this death drive, this aggression and destruction drive. This threat is *in-finite*, it sweeps away the logic of finitude and the simple factual limits, the transcendental aesthetics, one might say, the spatio-temporal conditions of conservation. Let us rather say that it abuses them. . . . Enlisting the in-finite, archive fever verges on radical evil.[10]

There you have it. First, the impetus for construction, memory, conservation: a course of German language study in the local schools supported with textbooks. The layers in operation here are deep and obvious: language, acquisition, repetition, conservation, memory. The study of German was appropriate: Menominee had a significant German-American population. Side-by-side existed, clearly, whether one chooses to dismiss Derrida (and Freud) or not, and whatever one may wish to call it, a "destruction drive" or "death drive" or "radical evil" that was made incarnate in the spectacle of burning German language textbooks. Needless to say,

German had just been dropped from the school curriculum. Today we have a local Archives, perhaps in need of an HVAC system, that conserves the evidence of the dual sides of "archive fever." We have the conservation of the evidence of destruction of that which was once conserved.

It might be useful to muse about the similarities between war fever and "archive fever." The same people who cheered wildly at the safe return of those Company L's soldiers who came home to Menominee in 1919 also encouraged children to brandish little American flags at the book burning.[11] These are two very different sides of the face of patriotism: the conserving, conservative, conservation side, and that of death and destruction.

War fever was not the exclusive province of The American Club or there would have been no world war. This essay is one-sided in its presentation of American propaganda and is about that propaganda. This is not a commentary on the soldiers who killed and were killed. Also, and just as obviously, war also is not a temporal, temporary affliction. In the United States during World War I "Sauerkraut became liberty cabbage,"[12] just as French Fries became Victory Fries prior to the latest United States war in Iraq.

It is interesting that we chose the French as enemies, since we were not about to engage in combat with them. It seems as if we had more animosity towards the French than the so-called enemy. People were pouring out good wine and trampling French bread in the streets.[13] A local owner of a French restaurant received phone calls telling her to remove the French flag from the outside of her building. These are my memories, my impressions.

But there is a point to my bavarding. Stephane Audoin-Rouzeau and Annette Becker write that "what struck" Freud during World War I, "was that fear and hatred could develop and culminate in aggression even when similarities were stronger than differences."[14] Both Germany and France were convinced they were right. France looked at the war as a struggle between civilization and barbarism. Germany viewed France and England with their colonies as hypocrites. The war was viewed as one between races: the German and the French. That the French also used colonial troops (some of whom, by the way, fought side-by-side in the French 6th Army with Company L soldiers) was proof to the Germans of French "depravity."[15]

Today when one is required to indicate on forms her generalized European heritage, the idea of separate French and German races is ludicrous. "We should perhaps suggest," write Audoin-Rouzeau and Becker, "that the entire culture of war may rest on a kind of narcissism, turning minor distinctions into major areas of contention, with symbolic elements all the more important because the real differences are insignificant."[16] It seems to me that this is really why many of us common citizens went after France a few years back.

Oh sure, I have heard it said on the street that the French do not work as hard as we do. They are lazy, enjoy long vacations, and like to sit around in the sunshine and drink coffee out of tiny real cups. They don't have enough McDonalds's and take-away coffee. And, after all, we bailed them out of both World War I and World War II.

Is not all this anecdotal "evidence" against France proof that Freud was right, that Audoin-Rouzeau and Becker are right, proof of little differences in a sea of similarity? My impression is that we have much more antipathy today for the French than we do for the Germans, whom we hated so much in 1918 (and, of course, later). But we elected the French to be our enemies not only because they are an easy target, but precisely because they were not the problem.[17] For the French could not really keep us from waging war in Iraq if we were determined to do so, as we proved. And we did not at the time know our enemies well enough to hate them (although we had experience that led us to fear them).[18] We were not close enough to them; before the 2004 American election we (ok, many of us) even confused Saddam Hussein with Osama bin Laden and Iraq with Al-Qaeda.

What was behind the American Club's book burning? Menominee was filled with Americans of German extraction and with evidence of German culture: the breweries, the churches, the language textbooks in the schools. Prior to World War I, in the Wisconsin Evangelical Lutheran Synod, that to which Christ Lutheran Church of Menominee belonged, "almost all church services and confirmation classes were still conducted in German."[19] This was underscored when I looked at records from the period at Christ Lutheran in 2005; the records were written in German. O'Hara's anxiety, if that is what it was, is understandable. It is not as if there were no grounds on which to perceive a threat for, as Jeremy Kilar writes,

> Efforts to preserve and take pride in things German experienced a popular revival not only in rural Michigan but especially among German urban intellectuals as World War I approached. . . . These activities often were led by the National German-American Alliance, a loose federation of over three million members in forty states. Originally founded as a league to fight prohibition legislation [a battle lost in 1919], it was financed by brewers and led by businessmen, clergy, journalists, and educators. In Michigan, the Alliance vigorously promoted the use of the German language, German newspapers, and parochial schools; it gathered considerable support in both urban and rural German communities.[20]

But my point is not about a threat, or the misguided perception of one, but about proximity, closeness. Any perceived threat should have lessened as war approached. As Kilar notes, "despite the efforts of these pro-German elements, thousands of German Americans in Michigan shifted toward supporting intervention [on the side of the Allies] as war clouds gathered." This did not, however, stop the O'Hara's of this world. "Nonetheless," writes Kilar, "anti-German sentiment was already ingrained within the state, and once the United States entered the war, efforts were energized to repress opposition and to Americanize foreign-born nationalities." It was in this context that the Menominee book burning took place, anti-German propaganda accelerated, and the war was reported as Menominee waited for news of Company L.[21]

Articles about the book burning appeared in the newspaper days before the event took place and weeks before Company L saw any serious action in the war. That action came soon enough. As part of the 32nd (Red Arrow)

Division, Company L had their baptism of fire on July 31 during the Second Battle of the Marne (or Aisne-Marne offensive).[22]

On that date, Company L was a lead element in an assault on the German machine gun positions on Hill 212. After initial confusion and surprise, the company fought doggedly, but the wheat fields, hills, and woods near Sergy and Cierges were a killing ground for the company. Company L lost thirty-two enlisted men and one officer killed in action — out of roughly 200-215 soldiers — in that single day of fighting. Of the fifty-five-to-sixty men in the company from Menominee, nine were killed on July 31. In late August, 1918, the deaths of five of these local Company L soldiers killed in the Second Battle of the Marne were announced in the *Herald-Leader*, and shortly thereafter, a sixth was added to the list. Of these six soldiers, memorial services for three were held at Christ Lutheran church, "formerly the German Lutheran church."[23] In addition, the death of John Teichler of Company L, one of the nine soldiers from Menominee killed at Hill 212, had yet to be reported. Obviously, Menominee's German Americans had proven themselves worthy, if dying in battle constituted proof.

During the month between July 31 and the news of the Hill 212 battle deaths, the *Herald-Leader* carried articles daily on the great Aisne-Marne battle and other aspects of the war. "Americans Hold Their Own in Fiercest Battle," read the headlines on July 30; and beneath that heading, "Germans Made Most Determined Effort in Entire Battle in Chateau Thierry to Dislodge Yankees from Their Position North of the Ourcq."[24]

While this article had the situation a trifle twisted — Allied (Entente) forces were then making a most determined effort to dislodge the Germans from positions north of the Ourcq — news of The Second Battle of the Marne was reaching the U.S. in timely fashion. On July 31 the *Herald-Leader* noted the arrival of the Rainbow (42nd) Division at the front.[25] A subheading for an article on August 1 surmised correctly, "Huns May Go to Vesle."[26] On August 2 the people of Menominee read a statement that historians still corroborate: "Tide of War Now Turned."[27]

By August 3, the *Herald-Leader* reported "Local Companies Now in Midst of Immense Battle." "Company L of Menominee, and Company I, of Marinette [Wisconsin][28] are now taking part in the big battle along the Aisne-Marne front," the story continued. "Gen. March, chief of staff . . . announced that the 32nd Division, made up mostly of Michigan and Wisconsin troops, and the 42nd Division, were brought up to reinforce the other six divisions in the counter offensive on the Crown Prince's army."[29]

Menominee now knew their boys were in the thick of the struggle. Articles accurately mentioned Sergy and Cierges as a locale of the fighting.[30] Tension that mounted as townspeople waited to see how the local boys had fared reached the breaking point as the entire month of August passed without definite news of Company L.

While the citizens of Menominee watched for word of the local soldiers, there was no shortage of anti-German propaganda in the *Herald-Leader* or, for that matter, anti-German sentiment in the city. In the rhetoric of the time, Germans were rarely just Germans, at least not in the headlines: they were the Huns, the Boche(s). Of course, this name-calling had disparate meanings. When reporters used those words, they often seemed to do so with particular vehemence. The tone of soldiers using these words varied from hatred to tongue-in-cheek.

In fact, the Germans were de-humanized in the local press to the extent that the *Herald-Leader* reported Company L's first killing of a German soldier as if the killer were a hunter and the killed, an animal. A July 29 piece entitled "Menominee Boys Proud of Feat of Jessel," stated that "Charles Jessel, Jr., 22 years old . . . 612 Pearson avenue [Menominee] . . . is the first member of Company L . . . to have the honor and distinction of killing a boche. . . . The news of Jessel's achievement in 'getting' the first Hun was not told by him. He is too modest, and too much engrossed in the big battle to think of writing about his own laurels."[31]

Instead, another Menominee soldier, Felix Trudell, who served with the 125th's headquarters company, relayed the information of the first kill in a letter to his brother published in the July 29 article. The *Herald-Leader* reporter wrote that Trudell "told of Jessel's achievement and how it made Jessel one of the most popular men in the company."[32]

Trudell's own words, had one bothered to read them, were restrained when compared with the reporter's commentary that had preceded the published letter. Trudell wrote, "Charles Jessell, from Finntown, was the first man in Company L to kill a German. I was coming out of the trenches when I met Company L going in. Gee, I was glad to see them. But I just had time to say hello and good-bye."[33] Trudell wrote nothing about Jessell's relative popularity and even used the word "German."

This did not stop the *Herald-Leader* from printing a photograph of Jessel and telling again of his amazing feat — and not just once, either. On August 5, the paper displayed a picture of Jessel beneath the caption, "Menominee Boy First in Co. L to Kill a Hun."[34] And even as late as early 1919, with the war ended, the same photograph of Jessel, who posed with Company L buddy Raymond Kubiak, appeared in the *Herald-Leader*. This time the caption read, "He Got One! Menominee Boy Who is Said to Be the First Member of Company L to Bag a Boche."[35]

As Menominee waited for news of Company L, the war — for the American soldier, at least — was portrayed in the press as a relatively safe and healthy endeavor. An article in the August 5 edition of the newspaper proclaimed that "Fewer Than One in 20 Dies From Wounds in Battle."[36] On August 6, the *Herald-Leader* printed "Casualty List Must Be Viewed Conservatively," which advised that "'wounded, degree not determined,' may mean a very slight wound as well as one of a more serious nature."[37] These items were meant to reassure the citizens of Menominee as they waited for word from the front. The latter article, not coincidentally, was meant to allay fears as the government released the first news of wounded soldiers from Marinette.

Probably the height of what we would now, perhaps, call irony appeared when, on August 10, the newspaper printed a lengthy syndicated article replete with cartoon illustrations, whose headline above a sketch of a smiling doughboy read, "'Your Sons Safe in Army Camps,' Is Message to American Mothers." Beneath an illustration of the happy soldier, another caption: "Don't Worry! — He is All Right!"[38]

The part about being safe in camp was true, as far as it went, at least prior to the onset of the influenza pandemic in the autumn of 1918 (an earlier round of the flu had been less virulent). With the flu came death in droves from pneumonia, even in stateside camps. There was no safe place, as a soldier or citizen. Entire families were wiped out, or nearly so.

The army also tried to downplay this danger for as long as possible, and used the local press to help. "Camp Custer Notes" in the October 10 *Herald-Leader* observed that the Augusta, Michigan army camp "set a new record for physical fitness of men received in any one month." As for the flu, "Officers at Camp Custer do not believe the prevalence of Spanish influenza in the cantonment should occasion any great worry among relatives and friends of the soldiers training there." Moreover, said the article, "The camp is extraordinary [sic] well equipped and prepared to combat the contagion and the number of cases developed is not relatively large."[39]

By the next day, facts forced the *Herald-Leader* to back away from these statements. Surprisingly enough, considering the pronouncements of the day before, the state board of health had put local health officers on alert. Further, it was noted, "The epidemic at Camp Custer seems to have been a 'real epidemic.'" In addition, "several deaths" were said to "have occurred."[40]

That was all the warning Menominee received. On October 12, the *Herald-Leader* reported that five men from Menominee city and county, all of whom had left for training on August 28, had died from influenza at Camp Custer.[41] *The Honor Roll of Menominee County* listed twelve men as having died from disease in the month of October alone.[42] That month, a distraught Colonel C. H. Hagadorn, acting commander at Camp Grant, Illinois, committed suicide. "'The cause of his death was due no doubt to a nervous collapse brought on by work and worry over the epidemic in camp,' said Col. Charles W. Castle."[43]

Nevertheless, in "'Your Sons Safe'" the army was portrayed as the ultimate training ground in every way. "Regardless of the opinion of doting mother," the article continued, "many boys grow up self-centered, lazy, bigoted, and without high moral standards. Military discipline will correct these faults soon." Mothers everywhere were assured that "Your boy is working hard. He is playing hard. He is living out in the open." Today, of course, this sort of cant sounds more like a good western than the Western Front, with its lice, filth, and constant danger.[44]

Or does it? How different is the 1918 article from the long-running "Be All That You Can Be" recruiting campaign? Nor does the World War I view vary greatly from the more recent "Army of One" advertisements. The ads say, "With technology, with training, with support, who I am has become better than who I was." From 1918 to today, self-improvement has been the crux of the army's message.

Captions beneath cartoon vignettes accompanying "'Your Sons Safe'" read: "Food is Abundant and Wholesome; The Average Boy Will Come Out of the Army Better Mentally Than Before He Went In; Everything is Done to Build Up Perfect Physical Manhood; The Y.M.C.A. Huts are Always Open to Your Boy; The Death Rate in the Army is Less Than it is in Civilian Life."[45]

Of course, even the army could not guarantee absolutely the safety of soldiers who might, for some reason, such as a battle, leave the beneficent environs of camp. And lest this unhappy reminder of mortality dampen enthusiasm for the army's program of self-improvement, the writer of the article had a few reassuring words about casualties: "You may read soon — probably before this is published, lists from the battle front of American boys killed or wounded. If the numbers seem great and cause anxious fear to clutch your heart, remember that we are dealing in vast figures. Compared with the number of men involved the casualties will show proportionately very small."[46]

This was true also, as far as it went. According to a table derived from J.M. Winter's *The Great War and the British People* in Niall Ferguson's *The Pity of War*, the "total" of United States soldiers "killed as a percentage of total mobilized" was a mere 2.7 percent. These figures, of course, pale when compared with Germany (15.4%), France (16.8%), Britain and Ireland (11.8%), or Scotland (26.4%).[47]

On the other hand, an estimated 114,000-126,000 United States soldiers died in World War I in approximately 200 days of fighting (see Essay 1, note 14). In late July 1918, Company L was on the front lines in the Aisne-Marne offensive. On July 31 when Company L and the 3rd Battalion of the 125th Infantry Regiment attacked uphill against machine gun emplacements, overall statistics became meaningless. And when news of casualties in the Aisne-Marne battle started to filter back to the United States, the townspeople of Menominee had to have been worried. This despite the happy injunction in "'Your Sons Safe'" that "The great majority of American boys who went over or are going over there will return to America, much healthier for having served abroad, more fitted to cope with the world, broadened, educated, and better suited to do their life work"[48]: the Great War glossed as equal parts dude ranch and finishing school.

On rare occasions, the *Herald-Leader* provided balance. One such example, with an Ann Arbor dateline, "Soldiers Want a New Brand of Christianity," was a refreshingly frank discussion of the war's impact on religion and a remarkable departure from the typical war rhetoric. Eschewing platitudes, The Reverend Perry Atkins, head of the Y.M.C.A.'s national war work council maintained that many of the men who fought in the war were through with phony piety.[49]

Atkins had been gassed in France and had returned home to discuss a pragmatic religion based not on show but on action, not on differences but on common humanity, a religion not of faith but of works, with a bit of millennialist optimism thrown in for good measure. "'Over there'," said Atkins, "it's not what a man does not do, but what he does that measures his worth. Jesus Christ was great not because he did not smoke cigarettes and drink but because of what he did."[50]

Compare "Soldiers Want New Brand of Christianity" with an item in the August 22 Herald-Leader in which some of the writings of Nietzsche are portrayed as the "German View of Christianity." "How much has his [Nietzsche's] philosophy affected the views and character of the Germans of today?" the writer of the article asks rhetorically. "Is not the answer written in the blood of the women and children and the old men of occupied France and Belgium?"[51]

In his passionate style, Nietzsche is quoted: "I condemn Christianity. To me it is the greatest of all imaginable corruptions. The church is the great parasite; with its anemic idea of holiness it drains life of all its strength, its love, and its hope. The other world is the motive for the denial of every reality."[52] Except for the bit about condemning Christianity as the greatest of all imaginable corruptions, Nietzsche sounds curiously like Perry Atkins of Newton, Kansas.

One letter that was printed after war's end while anti-German sentiment was still very strong countered for an instant the fairly steady stream of propaganda. In January 1919, The *Herald-Leader* printed a letter from Merritt "Tug" Wilson to Menominee's Frank Seidl that actually praised the Germans as fighters. Wilson had long been Captain Oscar Falk of Menominee's right hand with Company L.[53] Now Wilson was in Germany.

During World War I, Falk was assigned to command Company F of the 125th Infantry (the same regiment as Company L); Wilson, too, was transferred from L at Falk's behest. Falk was mortally wounded on July 31 at les Jomblets, Hill 212, but Wilson survived the war intact — almost. During one encounter, a German shell had exploded near Wilson, throwing him twenty feet into the air. "When I woke up," Wilson told Seidl, "I was in the hospital."[54]

When Sergeant Ralph Brown of Marinette's Company I, 127th Infantry, returned home on leave in September, 1918, he told the *Herald-Leader* that Wilson "was thrown several feet in the air and landed on his head. Some time ago, Lieut. Wilson had a steel tube put in his head, due to some injury he received in private life, and when he landed he struck his head near the tube, breaking both eardrums."[55]

This was only partially or, perhaps, half true. In a letter to his father and sister published in the *Herald-Leader*, Wilson remarked that "I got hit with a big chunk of mud along side of the left ear. . . . It put that bum ear of mine out altogether. It was not much good before, but it is no good at all now. But that don't make any difference. I have one good ear left, and that is one too much for the boche."[56]

Another encounter left Wilson, as he told Seidl, with "one of my big toes shot about half off." With only one good leg, Wilson could not keep up with his company and soon became an easy target for German machine gunners. He had, naturally, sought cover and jumped into a shell hole only to find that the enemy soldiers in the same hole greatly outnumbered him.[57]

"Well, say," Wilson told Seidl, "maybe you think that there wasn't something doing in that shell hole. You know, Fin, old boy, that I can move around a little when I have to. For a few seconds, I forgot all about being hit and I just moved everything I had, but if a few of the boys had not come back after me, well maybe I would not be writing to you now." Decorated for bravery in the war, Wilson had been reported dead several times. He spoke with authority, then, when he told Seidl, "But, say Fin, don't let anyone tell you that Fritz can't fight, for he can all right." Wilson even had good things to say about Germany itself. "Say, but this is some country, while you're talking. No wonder it took the whole world to lick the old boy."[58]

More typical of the articles that appeared in the *Herald-Leader* were those such as that printed upon the return of Sergeant Brown. These items portrayed the Germans as unfair, cowardly, and amoral, for starters. At the same time, either implicitly or explicitly, American soldiers were depicted as clean-living, fair-fighting, and brave. The tone and substance of most of the local newspaper pieces on the war tended to sway between complaints about the Germans and righteous or self-righteous braggadocio.

"'Oh those dastardly, contemptible Huns," Brown told the Herald-Leader. "No one but he who has actually gone through the front-line, met those yellow pups face to face, can even conceive what an enemy the civilized world is facing."[59]

In a letter published in the *Herald-Leader*, Sergeant-Major Martin Ferry observed that "The German soldiers are very savage and they do everything to destroy this country, France. There is no word too strong to express the feelings of the allies' soldiers against the Germans. The German soldiers are just like savages in their fighting, but the war will soon be over, with a victory won."[60]

By contrast, a September 9 article recounted, through the eyes of Corporal Harry Allard, the Hill 212 assault and the 32nd Division's ensuing "Drive from the Ourcq to the Vesle." The subheading of the article stressed the religious nature of the Menominee soldiers (as well as their precarious situation): "Menominee Boys Pray to God as They Charged Through a Veritable Hell on July 31."[61]

If anything, the tone of newspaper articles — both local and from the news services — became even more bellicose as months passed. A November 5 headline advised that "Maligners of Red Cross Should be Shot At Sunrise: This is the Way . . . Pro-German Liars Ought to be Treated."[62] Newspaper snippets such as "Bismarck, N.D. wants to change its name. We'd be ashamed of it if it didn't,"[63] and "Huns Took Charity Money," kept war fever high.[64] On October 8, the *Herald-Leader* reported that "The voice of the nation, as heard in congress, is practically unanimous against any parley with the foe until he has been smashed into helplessness. . . . This feeling is stronger in the middle west than anywhere else."[65]

In essence, The Allies were portrayed as fighting for all that was good: God, Freedom, Democracy, "Universal Culture,"[66] and even Little Belgium. Belgium, a neutral country, had been invaded by the Germans at the beginning of the war. The Germans surely committed atrocities. Even officers in the German army objected to the use of poison gas in warfare.[67] But no one mentioned, as Niall Ferguson suggests, that "if Germany had not violated Belgian neutrality in 1914, Britain would have."[68] No one mentioned the slaughter in the Belgian Congo that had gone on for decades.[69] No one mentioned the atrocities committed on the Allied side because they were convinced that the Germans were barbarians, a product of localized German *Kultur*, the antithesis of "universal culture": in a word, evil. Thus, whatever measures taken against them were justified. No one on the Allied side flinched at the killing of Germans. This was a war that produced very few pacifists. As Audoin-Rouzeau and Becker put it, "pacifists were as rare between 1914 and 1918 as they were legion after the war."[70]

And once in battle, soldiers of the 32nd Division, some spurred with thoughts of revenge, fought ferociously. When Sergeant Lyle Cole started up Hill 212,

> Sergeant Wojezechowski, over on my left, called to me, 'Let's give them hell Cole'. . . . The next time I looked back Wojezechowski threw up his hands, dropped his rifle, whirled around, and fell to the ground. He was a good friend of mine, and a fine chap. It is impossible to describe my feelings. It made me so mad all I could think of was getting to the top and getting at those Dutch bastards.[71]

Sergeant Brown recalled the Aisne-Marne battle:

> Those seven days I will never forget. It was awful. We saw our own comrades and friends fall. Some were awful sights. You may think it strange for a person who just a year ago was enjoying all the peace loving qualities of the American republic, to go to France and actually take the life of one of the enemy, but I tell you there is not a single reflection on one's conscience when he does it. If you would see some friend lying on the battlefield, with several bullets through his body, you forget everything but the idea of getting the first German you come across and believe me, we got them good and proper.[72]

Besides the usual causes for which the Americans were fighting, articles in the *Herald-Leader* even promoted the chestnut of defending women from the ravages of the enemy. "We passed through a village that the Germans had vacated during our advance," Sergeant Brown said in a speech to the Chamber of Commerce of Marinette, "and the Germans had over 30 women naked in a church."[73] Apparently, it was not bad enough that the women were simply naked; they were disrobed in a place of worship. Naturally, "The Americans put guards around the church," Brown continued, "sent for clothes and clothed the women and sent them back to the villages where they reside."[74]

By the middle of August, local casualties from companies other than L were announced in the *Herald-Leader*. First, Michael Hoefer of Marinette and Company I, killed in action.[75] Sergeant Brown reported in September that Hoefer "received a one-pounder in his left side. . . . His whole side was torn away."[76] Then on August 16, the *Herald-Leader* announced the deaths of I Company's Sergeant Fred Murray of Menominee and Company C of the 127th's Antonio Kossewski, of Wallace in Menominee County.[77] Kossewski was listed as having been killed in action; Murray as having died of wounds. Brown later explained that Murray "received five bullets, and after lying on the ground, received two more. He died after they brought him to the field hospital."[78] At this point, the fate of Company L was still unknown, but there was now real cause for worry.

Finally, on August 28, the suspense about Company L cracked. "Five Members of Co. L, Menominee, Die Fighting for Liberty's Cause," the *Herald-Leader* trumpeted. "City is Bowed in Mourning for its Brave Young Heroes," the headlines continued. "First Casualties Reported from Company L Hit Menominee a Severe Blow. Wild, Exaggerated Rumors Immediately Follow Report of Sad News from Front, All Without Foundation."[79]

The five reported dead were Peter Boivin, Harold Johnson, William Baker, John Stauber, and Walter Pada. Obituaries and photographs of "The Five Menominee Heroes Who Fell in Battle July 31st" appeared in the same issue. "The heavy toll on Menominee recorded in last night's messages," the article went on, "caused wild rumors to quickly spread throughout the Twin Cities [Menominee and Marinette; not St. Paul and Minneapolis] during the night and this morning, some saying that 17 men were killed, while others claiming that the entire company was annihilated." Such rumors were, of course, "false, as the five messages to the relatives of the foregoing men were all that were received."[80]

But the rumors of more dead were not entirely false. During the next few days, news trickled in of the deaths of the four other soldiers killed on July 31: first, Arthur Lueskow;[81] then, Albert Johnson and Fred St. Peter;[82] and finally, Sergeant John Teichler.[83] Their obituaries varied in content and tone from expected details to surprise angles.

For example, Mechanic Fred St. Peter of Company L was posthumously criticized for not writing to his mother. "That the announcement of his death should be the first message the parents have received from him gives his supreme sacrifice . . . an added pathos," St. Peter's obituary read.[84]

By the time he finished with St. Peter, the obituary writer might well have substituted "bathos" for "pathos." "He [St. Peter] arrived in France late in February," the article went on, "and since that time, his parents have not received a single word from him. Daily the heart-broken mother watched for the mail carrier, expecting a message from her son, but none came." Fortunately for the dead St. Peter, his reputation was partly restored when the obituary stated that despite his apparent lack of concern for the welfare of his mother he was "a fine example of American manhood."[85]

Even more time had passed before Lena Falk learned of her husband's death. Oscar Falk's death was not officially reported until October 23, though foreboding rumors had filled the local papers for months.[86] Falk, the former Company L Commander, had led Company F on July 31 in an assault on les Jomblets in front of Cierges and had been wounded in action. He died on August 1, less than two weeks before his 54th birthday. If Lena Falk could take solace, it was, said "Tug" Wilson, in that "god took him away. Because he did not want him to go through the hell that the rest of us did afterwards. For that is all it was. . . . I often said that I was glad that poor old dad was at rest. And not have to be in the hell that we were."[87]

Oscar Falk's remains were finally brought home and reburied in

Menominee's Riverside Cemetery in September 1921. It had taken Mrs. Falk three frustrating years to get the body of her husband back from France. Grover Thompson, another longtime member of Company L, was given a prominent role in the funeral.[88]

Thompson had joined Company L while still in his teens. The thin lieutenant, still young at thirty-one, had taken command of Company L in August 1918 following the 32nd Division's "Drive from the Ourcq to the Vesle." The company commander, Captain John McCabe, who had led L into battle on July 31, suffered a nervous breakdown, according to Company L Corporal John Daley[89]; Thompson said McCabe's "sore eyes," probably from a gas attack, had left the captain incapacitated.[90] Lieutenant Charles Hammond of Company L had been killed at Hill 212; another lieutenant had been shell-shocked. A fourth officer was detached from the company for training. By the end of August, Thompson was the only officer with Company L.[91]

Thompson commanded Company L through the rest of the war, through the Oise-Aisne and Meuse-Argonne campaigns. He presided over a company that had been decimated in battle. By the end of August, Company L's strength was reported at just 102 men, roughly half of the number that had fought at Hill 212 on July 31.[92] In 1921, Thompson led the funeral cortege for his commander from the orange-bricked Presbyterian Church, down Ogden Avenue (now 10th Avenue), to a train of trolley cars and, finally, to the cemetery and the shade of maples near the banks of the Menominee River.

---

[1]Senior English Class of 1925, "History of Menominee, 1910-1925," MCHS-ARC.

[2]"American Club Plans Monster Demonstration," *HL*, June 12, 1918. See also "Burning of Books to Follow Patriotic Parade," *HL*, June 15, 1918.

[3]"Thousands to See German Books Burn," *HL*, June 17, 1918.

[4]"American Club Plans Monster Demonstration," June 12, 1918.

[5]Obituary of Augustus Spies, *HL*, August 14, 1915.

[6]"Great Throng Rejoices as Books Burn," *HL*, June 18, 1918.

[7]"Address at Book Burning Made Tremendous Hit," *HL*, June 18, 1918. Whenever I think about the Menominee book burning, I am reminded of the words of David Mamet: "Our World Position is not tenuous, but our mental balance is. In our devotion to the ideas of our own superiority, we are like compulsive gamblers who destroy themselves by enacting a drama of their own worthlessness." Mamet, *Three Uses of the Knife*, 45. Actually, I could write an entire essay on

Mamet's argument and the book burning. But it well may be that enacting too many such dramas can and will actually cause our World Position to become tenuous.

[8]Of course, the German textbooks fail some of the tests of archival documents as we sometimes understand them today. The books probably had no contextual, idiosyncratic, finding aids. They are not records of an organization or an activity of an organization or an office or someone's personal papers. They were not housed in an archival institution. There obviously were many copies about. They meet other standards: outwardly kept, legally supported, and so forth. I speak of archives writ large. Further, I meet O'Hara on his own terms. He spoke of sending the books to the "archives of hell," not the library of hell. Perhaps he should have considered sending only one copy.

[9]Derrida, *Archive Fever*, 11-12. This was a point made in the context of the longer University of Illinois thesis. Other examples of the archive (writ large) "working against itself" in the case of remembering Company L have occurred over time. One such example appears in the notes to this book: that of the recently altered Company L display at Menominee's Heritage Museum.

[10]Ibid., 19-20. And for the record, an elongated flame's image graces the dustjacket of Archive Fever.

[11]"Thousands to See German Books Burn," HL, June 17, 1918. A passage reads: "All school children and all others taking part in the parade are requested to carry American flags."

[12]Braun, *Together in Christ*, 27. Writes Jeremy Kilar, even "German Measles became 'Liberty Measles'." Kilar, *Germans in Michigan*, 38.

[13]This is as foolish as burning German textbooks. Here allow me to interject a note of levity into all this gravity. If my fellow Americans didn't want the French wine, I would have been happy to take it off their hands.

[14]Audoin-Rouzeau, 14-18, 150.

[15]Ibid. 142-158. And proof to us today of German (and human) depravity.

[16]Ibid., 150.

[17]As Mamet says, "Racist America elected African Americans The Villain. Once elected, that race suffered not because it was the cause of the whites' unrest, but because it was *not*. Christian Europe elected Jews the cause of its distress, and fury against the Jews mounted as each pogrom proved unrewarding. Anti-Semitism flourishes today in Germany, a country virtually devoid of Jews." Mamet, *Three Uses of the Knife*, 52.

[18]Of course, we were also placed in a difficult situation. Again these are but my own memories. We intended, we said, to liberate the people we were attacking. Thus it was harder to hate them as is usually done. So someone had to take the heat: France, I guess.

[19]Braun, *Together in Christ*, 27.

[20]Kilar, *Germans in Michigan*, 36-37.

[21]Ibid., 38.

[22]See Essay 1.

[23]"Memorial Rites to be Said for 3 Co. L Heroes," *HL*, August 30, 1918. Also, see "Solemn Services to be Held for Menominee Heroes," *HL*, August 31, 1918. The three soldiers were William Baker, Arthur Lueskow, and Walter Pada. Baker's mother's name was Alvina Becker; it is possible that William had Americanized his name. See several documents in Baker, William, file folder not numbered; MN-81, E-1942, HM 1997; "Burial Case Files"; Cemeterial Division; RG 92; NACP.

[24]"Americans Hold Their Own in Fiercest Battle," *HL*, July 30, 1918.

[25]"Rainbow is Now 'In'," *HL*, July 31, 1918.

[26]"Allies Straighten Line; Pave Way to Flank Enemy," *HL*, August 1, 1918.

[27]"Huns Withdraw in Defense and Yanks Sweep On," *HL*, August 2, 1918.

[28]Company I of Marinette, Wisconsin, like Company L, had been a National Guard unit. Company I formed part of the 127th Infantry Regiment, 64th Brigade, in the 32nd Division.

Menominee and Marinette are "twin cities" separated by the Menominee River.

[29]"Local Companies Now in Midst of Immense Battle," *HL*, August 3, 1918.

[30]See, for example: "Huns Pit Best Troops Against U.S. Soldiers," *HL*, July 29, 1918; "Rainbow is now 'In'," *HL*, July 31, 1918.

[31]"Menominee Boys Proud of Feat Done by Jessel," HL, July 29, 1918.

[32]Ibid.

[33]Ibid.

[34]"Menominee Boy First in Co. L to Kill a Hun," *HL*, August 5, 1918;

[35]"He Got One!", HL, February 4, 1918.

[36]"Fewer Than One in 20 Dies From Wounds in Battle," *HL*, August 5, 1918.

[37]"Casualty List Must Be Viewed Conservatively," *HL*, August 6, 1918.

[38]"'Your Sons Safe in Army Camps'," *HL*, October 10, 1918.

[39]"Camp Custer Notes," *HL*, October 10, 1918. Augusta is near Battle Creek.

[40] "Epidemic Hits State Lighter Than Others," *HL*, October 11, 1918.

[41]"Death Toll of Menominee Men at Custer is 5," *HL*, October 12, 1918.

[42]Herald-Leader Company, *Honor Roll*, 22-23.

[43]"Commander at Camp Grant Commits Suicide," *HL*, October 8, 1918.

[44]"'Your Sons Safe in Army Camps'," *HL*, October 10, 1918.

[45]Ibid.

[46]Ibid.

[47]Ferguson, *Pity of War*, 299.

[48]"'Your Sons Safe in Army Camps'," *HL*, October 10, 1918.

[49]"Soldiers Want New Brand," *HL*, July 25, 1918.

[50]Ibid.

[51]"German View of Christianity," *HL*, August 22, 1918.

[52]Ibid.

[53]"Lieut. Wilson Writes Letter," *HL*, January 25, 1919.

[54]Ibid.

[55]"Sergt. R. Brown Home from Front with More News," *HL*, September 25, 1918. The 127th was part of the 64th Brigade in the 32nd Division.

[56]"Capt. Falk, Sick, Could Not Stand Shock of Wound," *HL*, September 27, 1918.

[57]"Lieut. Wilson Writes Letter," *HL*, January 25, 1919.

[58]Ibid.

[59]"Sergt. R. Brown Home from Front with More News," *HL*, September 25, 1918.

[60]"Menominee Boy Describes Hun Soldier Traits," October 15, 1918.

[61]"Company L in Terrific Battle for Eight Days," *HL*, September 9, 1918.

[62]"Maligners of Red Cross Should be Shot at Sunrise," *HL*, November 5, 1918.

[63]"Bismarck, N.D. wants to change its name," *HL*, August 22, 1918.

[64]"Huns Took Charity Money," *HL*, August 22, 1918.

[65]"America Shows Temper Toward German Peace," October 8, 1918.

[66]See Audoin-Rouzeau, *14-18*, "Civilisation, Barbarism, and War Fervour," especially 134-158. "Universal Culture," from the French point-of-view was French humanistic culture by definition. German Kultur, by definition, was sectarian: non-universal, limited to the barbaric German nation. It is interesting to note all the 1918 articles that trumpet the virtues of the French people in the *Herald-Leader*, the polar opposite of the popular view one frequently hears today.

[67]Ibid., 155.

[68]Ferguson, *Pity of War*, 67.

[69]Morrow, Jr., The Great War: *An Imperial History*, 8. "Between 1880 and 1920," writes Morrow, "Belgian atrocities—slave labor, plunder, the murderous suppression of rebellion,

attendant famine—depopulated the Congo by half, from 20 million people to 10 million people." Of course, part of the reason this was not an issue was race. And, as mentioned previously, the Germans argued, according to Audoin-Rouzeau and Becker, that the French were waging an uncivilized war because they used French colonial soldiers.

[70]*14-18,* 139.

[71]Cole, "1918 Diary," 37.

[72]"Sergt. R. Brown Home from Front with More News," *HL*, September 19, 1918.

[73]"Sergt. Brown Tells of Scenes on Battlefields," *HL*, September 25, 1918.

[74]Ibid.

[75]"Michael Hoefer, Member Co. I, Killed in Action," *HL*, August 15, 1918.

[76]"Sergt. R. Brown Home from Front with More News," *HL*, September 19, 1918.

[77]"Farmer Boy Dies a Hero Fighting Against Germany," *HL*, August 16, 1918; "Fred Murray Makes Supreme Sacrifice for US," *HL*, August 16, 1918.

[78]"Sergt. R. Brown Home from Front with More News," *HL*, September 19, 1918.

[79]"Five Members of Company L," *HL*, August 28, 1918.

[80]Ibid.

[81]"Memorial Rites to be Said for 3 Co. L Heroes," *HL*, August 30, 1918.

[82]"Corp. Albert Johnson Falls in Recent Fight," *HL*, September 4, 1918; "Another Co. L Boy Killed in Recent Battle," *HL*, September 4, 1918. Johnson was reported as having been killed on August 4, but he died in the Hill 212 battle on July 31.

[83]"Football Star is Killed While Helping Mate," *HL*, September 7, 1918.

[84]"Another Co. L Boy Killed in Recent Battle," *HL*, September 4, 1918.

[85]Ibid.

[87]"Capt. Oscar Falk Died of Wounds on August 1st," *HL*, October 23, 1918.

[87]Merritt Wilson to Lena (Mrs. Oscar) Falk, December 29, 1918, MCHS-ARC.

[88]"Final Rites of Oscar Falk Tomorrow P.M.," *HL*, September 3, 1921.

[89]"42 Co. L Boys Killed in Five Hours," *HL*, February 5, 1919

[90]"Lt. Thompson Now in Command of Company 'L'," *HL*, September 11, 1918.

[91]Ibid. Thompson was eventually promoted to captain.

[92]Strength Return, 125th Infantry, August, 1918; 125th Infantry 1917-1918, file folder not numbered; Infantry Regiments, 123 (Companies)-125; World War I Strength Returns; RG 407; NACP.

Essay 3

Company L and the "Burial Case Files"

Background

On July 31, 1918, nine soldiers from Menominee, Michigan, troops in Company L of the 125th Infantry Regiment of the 32nd Division, a unit attached to the French 6th Army, were killed in action in France. They died in the wheat fields and woods around Hill 212 near the village of Sergy north of Chateau-Thierry during the Second Battle of the Marne (Aisne-Marne offensive). "Burial Case Files"[1] for the nine men from Menominee and other soldiers killed in action are housed at the National Archives at College Park, Maryland. These records tell a harrowing story about the difficulties in caring for and identifying dead soldiers that the American Graves Registration Service (GRS) of the Quartermaster Corps (QMC) faced during World War I and that the Cemeterial Division of the Office of the Quartermaster General encountered after the war.[2] The files say something important, as well, about the form and process of making and keeping records that developed in World War I and its aftermath.

The character of the battle in which Company L fought on the last day of July and first week of August influenced the manner in which the soldiers were cared for. In the spring 1918 offensives, the German army had reached the Marne River, but their line formed what proved to be an untenable salient. A massive French counterattack that began on July 18 forced the German army back to successive lines of defense in depth, and front lines shifted steadily as the battle continued to rage. As the official history of the GRS put it, "the disappearance of graves was especially easy in Areas over which there was much fighting back and forth."[3]

The Menominee men were killed during the 32nd Division's assault on a defensive line constructed near the Ourcq River, a tributary of the Marne, as the Germans stubbornly fought in an organized withdrawal to a new line on the Vesle River at Fismes and Fismette. The men of the 32nd Division attacked from July 30 until they were relieved on August 6-7. For the first few days, each hill and woods was hotly contested. On the night of August 1-2 the Germans retreated to the Vesle. The 32nd Division pursued. The division advanced approximately eight-nine miles, captured Fismes on the south side of the Vesle, and was checked from crossing to the north bank.[4] Upon their relief from the front on August 6-7, the soldiers of the 32nd marched back and camped in the hills and woods they had fought so hard to gain. The bodies of their comrades — those who had not been hastily buried already — awaited them.

Paragraph 349 of the 1918 United States Army regulations dictated that "the dead are collected by details from the line as soon as practicable after the battle and disposed of as the commander directs."[5] But the fact of the matter was, in the opinion of the official history of the GRS, that "battle conditions make it impossible to bury men either decently or with any surety that their identity will be preserved."[6] Despite the Army regulations, "the physical inability of combatant Units to bury all their own dead" led the GRS to engage in "an exceedingly large and difficult amount of work in clearing battlefields, reinterring bodies and assembling them in selected spots."[7] This appears to be at odds with a later description in the history: "the [initial] burial of dead being by special orders a part of the duty of the combatant forces, no responsibility for the carrying out of this duty fell to the Graves Registration Service, but all burials were to be reported at once on grave location blanks in duplicate."[8] By the end of World War I, the GRS had assembled the bodies of 73,000 soldiers in "approximately one thousand different burial places."[9]

Upon going to war, the United States War Department had promised that "those men who fell should be returned to their homes, should their kin so desire."[10] Along with the nature of the war and individual battles mentioned above, "the unexpectedly large number of casualties"[11] the American Expeditionary Forces (AEF) suffered coupled with the learning curve that the

GRS faced made fulfilling this promise an onerous task if not a nightmare. Bodies either now needed to be shipped back to the United States or "concentrated" — often repeatedly — in larger cemeteries. Every such move had ramifications, not only in the physical world but in what was by then a virtual world of paper. In the process of attempting to make order out of chaos on the battlefields and cemeteries and within a growing bureaucracy, the GRS created documentation, much of it filled with redundant "facts" and with the possiblity of errors and misrepresentation.

The Records and the John Teichler File

I examined thirteen Burial Case Files from The National Archives at College Park. Along with the files of the nine soldiers from Menominee and Company L who were killed on July 31, I studied the burial file of Anton Johnson, brother of Company L's Albert Johnson; Anton had been transferred out of Company L to the 128th Infantry Regiment of the 32nd Division and was killed in action three days after Albert. I also perused the following records: those for Oscar Falk, longtime leader of Company L, who died on August 1; a second file for Company L's Peter J. Boivin (killed July 31) that was generated due to an alternative spelling of "Boivin" (Bovin); and the file of Arthur Faber, a soldier from Menominee who had suffered from shell shock. According to the US Army General Hospital 43, Report of Death, Faber hanged himself on July 8, 1919, in the National Soldiers' Home in Virginia.[12]

The following examples of documents from the file of Company L Sergeant John Teichler — and documents from other files discussed later in this essay — are not meant to be exhaustive, but suggestive, of the range of materials found in Burial Case Files. As cited in note one above, these files of the Cemeterial Division of the GRS from World War I contain as a chief organizing principle the "correspondence, reports, telegrams, applications, and other papers related to the burial of service personnel." Some files may even include physical objects such as identification tags in sealed envelopes (I never did open these).

The files include some documents without an official name — as far as I can tell — that are routinely present, such as the document that functions as John Teichler's Death Affidavit. This Death Affidavit included a brief account of how Teichler had died, an "Informant," the informant's home, and an officer's signature. The affidavit is not dated; none of the files I examined had dated affidavits. Teichler's Death Affidavit reads: "Killed in action on Chateau-Thierry front, July 31st 1918, at 3.00 PM on Hill No 212, near Sergy, France. Hit in breast by M.G. bullet while leading half platoon in the advance. Died instantly."[13]

Burial Case Files also include Reports of Disinterment and Reburial. The first such of these in Teichler's file, which I will call Report of Disinterment and Reburial (One) — or RDR1 — included the following items: name, rank and serial number of the disinterred soldier, his organization, date disinterred and reburied, location of disinterment and reburial, condition of body upon disinterment, identification tags or discs found on body (or on cross[14]), and instructions to send any personal effects to "the Effects Depot." This is the June 1919 version of the form as found in Teichler's file, created when he was exhumed nearly a year after his death from Cemetery #621, Grave 118, and supposedly reburied in Grave 250, Plot 5, Section H, Cemetery #608, Seringes-et-Nesles. This form includes a significant curiosity: the name typed on RDR1 is "David T. Davis." Teichler's name is written in cursive script and Davis' is crossed out. When this form was first filled out, the body in Cemetery 621, Grave 118 was thought to be that of David T. Davis.[15]

So just where was the body of John Teichler then? In July 1919, another unnamed record in memo form[16] from the Teichler file, which functioned as a Grave Location Form ("Location, Grave of"), represented the GRS's attempt to record information about and location of the body and grave in question. This document gives Teichler's name, rank, and serial number. The form then includes a list of queries: whether or not information on the deceased was accurate; "Date of death"; "Grave Location"; "Who reported burial?"; "Confirmed by G.R.S?"; "How is grave marked?"; "Identification tags: (a)

Buried with body? (b) Attached to grave Marker?"; "Emergency address"; and, referring to Emergency address, "Has been notified? (Give Date) [date given in this case was 12-5-19; thus, information was added to this record at a later time]." There is a space below for remarks and also to answer the following: "Requested by [left blank]," "European address," and "Checked by." This Grave Location Form asserted that Teichler had been reburied in Grave 252 of Plot 5, Section 6, Cemetery 608 at Seringes-et-Nesles.[17]

Teichler's file includes another Report of Disinterment and Reburial (Two) — RDR2 — from when the body in Grave 250, thought to be that of David Davis, was exhumed for purposes of identification on December 8, 1920. Next to the space for "complete location" of the disinterment was typed, "Grave 250, Section H, Plot 5, Cemetery No. 608," but next to "Grave 250" was handwritten a chilling if common finding: "Between grave 249 and [250]." This report included much of the same information as the first RDR, but with, in contrast to the RDR1 form, a dental diagram depicting 32 teeth with accompanying handwritten notes: dental records of the deceased. RDR2 also included more information in general concerning the body: height, weight, hair, hair on face, permanent marks on body, wounds or missing parts (received at time of casualty). For most of these categories, the answer on the form was a blanket "Impossible to determine" since the body was now "almost entirely decomposed."[18]

To the question on RDR1, "Was one identification tag found upon the body," the typed answer read, "No. None on cr [cross]."[19] On RDR2, item 5, "Identification tags: Buried with body?", the answer had now mysteriously become "Yes," and "Yes" on the grave marker. Further, under "other means of identification . . .and general remarks," the answer in RDR2 depicts what had now become a real mess: "Tag on cross reads: David T. DAVIS, Pvt., Co.D, 151 M.G. Bn. 114427. Tag on body, partly corroded: John ----O---, #263816 (plain)." In addition, item 6 (f), "Wounds or missing parts (received at time of casualty)," notes a "shell splinter in the head," a curious wound for a soldier who, according to the aforementioned Death Affidavit, was killed by a shot to the breast. At the top of the form, next to "Remains Of," "Teichler, John" was written in above the typewritten "Davis, David T.," and Teichler's serial number was written above Davis' crossed out serial number.[20]

In fact, an entire GRS investigation, ten pages in the Case of Private David T. Davis, is also included in the Teichler file; the Davis case is in the Teichler file for reasons that should, by now, be obvious. These papers include a request for disinterment, plus nine "Indorsements," or signed findings in the case, which was, of course, a case about determining — or attempting to — the identity of Davis, Teichler, and others.[21] The December 8, 1920 exhumation had been done in response to an October 1920 request to investigate the whereabouts of the body of Private Davis and a Private Fanus. For this reason two graves, including grave 250, plot 5, Section H, of Cemetery 608, were to be investigated.[22]

When grave 250 "was opened" in December 1920, "it was found that the cross marking this grave was midway between two bodies lying side by side. . . . The earth on either side was removed until it was found that one body was located directly beneath the cross marking grave 251, and another under the cross marking grave 249." This raised an issue: "Without uncovering the entire trench it is impossible to state which of the two bodies belonged under cross 250, or whether there are more bodies in this plot than there are crosses." Upon inspection, "an identification tag was found on the body" between crosses 250 and 251; the disc was that of Henry W. Grashoff. Between crosses 249 and 250 lay a body "which was doubled up in a bundle and almost entirely decomposed." The body had been "buried in uniform without a coffin" — as noted in RDR2 — and was found with Sergeant Teichler's number inscribed on a tag. The disc on the cross marking the grave and the cross itself both bore Davis' name.[23]

The 3rd Indorsement (January 6, 1921) in the Davis Case harkened back to the Teichler file's 1919 Grave Location Form, with the exception that Teichler was now located (on paper, that is) in Grave 252, section G (not section 6 — perhaps a "typo" in the Grave Location Form), Plot 5.[24] When the GRS exhumed Grave 252, Section G, Plot 5, "supposed to be the remains of John Teichler," according to the 4th Indorsement (January 12, 1921), uniform insignia on the corpse was that of Company I rather than Teichler's Company L.[25]

While Teichler's case was being investigated, another Information Sheet on the dead soldier was compiled in March 1921. This form included basic data such as the color of his hair and eyes, and his height and weight (when alive!).[26] An Identification Opinion form, dated two days after the Information Sheet, included dental information, information about the body, tags on the body, and other evidence: essentially the information, complete with anomalies, found in the Davis Case indorsements. More importantly, along with a statement of known "facts," a "Decision" was rendered: "The body of Sgt. Teichler is in this grave": "#250, Section H, Plot #5, Cty #608."[27]

But the matter was far from settled. On May 10, 1921, "Teichler" was exhumed yet again. This time, the body was disinterred from Grave 250, Section H, Plot 5 and moved to Grave 108, Section K, Plot 3; the body had been "given new gr. location for purpose of concentration."[28] The form for this Report of Disinterment and Reburial (Three), or RDR3, had not changed since RDR2. As in RDR2, RDR3 mentioned that "Disc on body read: John ------ 263816," but RDR3 also noted that "in reburial bottle: 16 – A read: 'DAVID T. DAVIS #114427.'" Apparently, the Davis disc had been removed from the cross and placed in a "reburial bottle" during the previous exhumation (?).[29] Decisions in the 5th (January 1921) and 7th (February 1921) Indorsements in the Davis case agreed, as did the 8th Indorsement, signed on May 14, 1921: the GRS deemed Sergeant Teichler's burial place Grave 250, Plot 5, Section H. Davis'/Teichler's RDR1 and RDR2 were evidently then retrieved and changed by hand to read "Teichler, John" instead of "Davis, David T." Documents in Davis' file became documents in Teichler's file. Of course, by the time the 8th Indorsement was written, the body in question had already been removed from Grave 250 and reburied in Grave 108, Section K, Plot 3.[30]

Return of "Sergeant Teichler"

"John Teichler's" exhumation in February 1922 for the purposes of shipping the body to Menominee resulted in yet another Report of Disinterment and Reburial (Four). This report was noteworthy for mentioning the following under the item, "Other means of identification found upon disinterment": "*Bottle record found in box agrees with GRS records* [my emphasis]."[31] This comment, in light of what we already know about the GRS records in John Teichler's file in general and RDR3 in particular is, if you will forgive me, exceedingly cryptic. By this time also, the numbers on the tag on the skeleton had corroded further: the disc now read merely "John – 3816."[32]

Also generated at this time was a Report of Disinterment, Preparation, and Shipment of Body. Under the section entitled "Comparative Report," the form noted that "No descrepancy" was "found upon examination of body" to indicate — at this time — that the remains were other than those of John Teichler. In this same form under "Discrepancy found upon disinterment," however, was a bit of an oddity. Once again, next to numbers 7 and 8 on the "Grave No." and "Sec." was typed a location that had been proven not to contain the body of Teichler in the investigations of late 1920 and 1921: "252" and "G." These were circled and "250" and "H" substituted by hand. On the second page of this form, many of the questions and answers reiterated RDR4. Under number 29, "Any discrepancy noted upon examinations of body, as compared with G.R.S. records quoted above," the soldier filling out the form typed, "See items 15 & 16 (over)." Items 15 and 16 referred to "Grave No. 108 Sec. K . . . Plot 3" and were in the "Discrepancy found upon disinterment" section near numbers 7 and 8. Bureaucratic mistakes hounded "John Teichler" well beyond the grave(s), but the GRS never seemed to quit their determined efforts to straighten these out.[33]

This second page also details to whom the body would be shipped and featured several entry spaces for shipping and receiving. Bodies of AEF soldiers were transported from cemeteries to "points of concentration," then shipped by barge and/or rail to Antwerp, and thence over the ocean to the

United States. Teichler's form was stamped as received in Antwerp on February 7, 1922. The body was shipped from the morgue in Antwerp on March 19, 1922 and arrived in Hoboken, New Jersey, on March 29, 1922.[34]

Two additional forms are in my copies from the NACP file: a Western Union telegram dated March 29, 1922 from Teichler's brother affirming that he wanted the body delivered to a local undertaker.[35] This was standard procedure and a final step in the process of delivering bodies to families of the deceased once they had been shipped to the United States. Another form, often the last in a burial case file, acknowledged receipt of the remains to the Quartermaster Supply Officer in Chicago a month later. Richard Lemieux, a Menominee undertaker, signed this form on April 29, 1922, nearly four years after the battle in which John Teichler had died.[36] According to a Michigan Department of Health form filed at Riverside Cemetery in Menominee, Teichler was buried for at least the fifth time the following day.[37]

Summary

John Teichler's labyrinthine case, unbelievable as it may seem, was not extraordinary. I noticed similar or even worse issues in many of the files I examined. Fred St. Peter's body was exhumed from a grave whose marker inscription read "Frank Murray."[38] Arthur Lueskow's file, which at first seems straightforward, turns into another maze. Lueskow's Report of Disinterment and Reburial (1919) lists discs as being found upon the body.[39] In 1921, another RDR noted that no tag was with the body and asserted that, in fact, "no actual identity established, only identification being disc and inscription on grave marker."[40]

John Stauber's file is exceptionally problematic. Again there were serious issues with identification. According to a Grave Location Form (One) from late 1918-early 1919, Stauber had been buried on the battlefield on August 2, 1918, two days after he died at Hill 212. He was then reburied in September 1918 in Grave 144, Row F of the American Battle Area Cemetery at Sergy.

According to this record — the questions on the form were typewritten and the answers written by hand — tags were buried with Stauber's body and placed on the cross marking his grave.[41] The location of the body and presence of identification bags on the body and cross were reiterated in a briefer, completely typed, Grave Location Form (Two) from around the same time.[42]

In a Report of Disinterment and Reburial dated June 16, 1919, Stauber's body was said to have been exhumed from Grave 144, Row F and reburied in Grave 274, Section E, Plot 6, of Cemetery 608.[43] Yet another Grave Location Form (Three) from July 1919 reflects this change. This form notes that Stauber was buried "8/2/19" [sic], but omits the September 1918 burial date recorded in Grave Location Form (One). Once again, this third Grave Location Form states that tags were reported to be on both body and cross.[44] But at some point something had gone terribly wrong.

Two documents from June 1921 detail the findings of the Board of Review that met at GRS Headquarters in Paris to examine "The case of Private John Stauber." In what was a masterly understatement, "The Board" was "of the opinion that there has been irregularity of burial in that section of the row in which this soldier was buried." The board found that "in Grave #274 [Section E., Plot 6, Cemetery 608] supposed to contain the remains of Pvt. John Stauber, body bearing no means of identification was found."[45]

At the same time, the board considered the case of "UNKNOWN U.S. SOLDIER. No. S.82" and determined that the body in nearby Grave 270, supposedly that of William C. Lempke, also could not be identified. Lempke's body was identified, however, by tag in Grave 273. In Grave 271, no body was found at all. Grave 272 also contained a body "bearing no means of identification." The Board of Review recommended that both cases be "referred to the Office of the Quartermaster General, Washington, D.C. for decision."[46] Nearly a year later, the decision was made in Washington: "By authority of Cable #1220 dated June 9th, 1922," the body that had once been in Grave 270, the "Unknown U. S. Soldier," whose body had been disinterred and moved twice within the space of three days in May 1921, was "ordered changed to 'Pvt. John Stauber, 263788, Co. L 125th Inf.'"[47] That is, what was left of the body. One Report of Disinterment and Reburial described the remains of "Unknown U.S. Soldier," now given an identity, whether true or false: "Skull Shattered. Skeleton from waist up, with exception of one Radius, missing."[48] The Report of Disinterment and Reburial from June 1919 that placed Stauber in Grave 274 was then changed by hand to read "270."[49]

Meanwhile, Michael Stauber, John's father, had asked that the body of his son be returned home, as reflected in two documents: a Shipping Inquiry and a Compilation of Disposition of Remains Data.[50] Mr. Stauber had diligently filled out all necessary forms and had even answered a December 1921 U.S. Army request from Washington for dental records, fractured bones, and the like. The query was ostensibly made "in order that the records of this office as regards your son, Private John Stauber . . . may be complete in all respects."[51] This approach was more than a trifle disingenuous given the Board of Review cases that were still undecided. The request is also puzzling, since an undated Information Sheet from Stauber's file already depicted his dental charts, supposedly based on the army's "physical report of examination prior to enlistment."[52] The body that was eventually said to be Stauber's was missing both the upper and lower jaw. Dental records would not have been much help in identifying that particular corpse.[53]

The record does not show to what degree Michael Stauber was informed of the investigations into his son's identity or whether he suspected the truth. Perhaps he just thought that things were taking a long time, as usual. Stauber wrote back: "I beg to advise you that my son had no dental work done with us before the War. I cannot remember any scar or mark that would serve as a means of identification. . . . This is also true relative to fractured bones. He was only sixteen years of age at the time of his enlistment and had no fractures previous to his entering the army."[54] The body of "John Stauber" did not arrive in Menominee until July 16, 1922.[55]

Of the seven of the nine Company L men from Menominee killed on July 31 who were sent home for burial, it was difficult to ascertain in nearly every case if the proper body had been sent home. Much paperwork supports the decisions that the GRS and Cemeterial Division made in these cases, but it would be interesting to know if families of the dead soldiers had the opportunity to view the files or portions thereof (and when) and what they would have thought and done as a result. I can only guess at these answers because I do not know. My guess is that much of the information in the files was off-limits to "non-authorized personnel," including (and, perhaps, especially) families. The Stauber file's Compilation of Disposition of Remains Data, for example — a document that lists, among other things, reburial sites — states repeatedly beneath the recorded grave locations, "This info. NOT to be released to N/R." Does N/R refer to "Nearest Relative," a formulation used commonly in the Burial Case File documents? Likely.[56]

The fears that families harbored — with good reason — are evident on another nameless form, a 3 x 5 card from the file of Harold Johnson that could be called "Request for Burial in the United States." The card asked several questions, including "relationship to the deceased," whether or not it was desired that the soldier's body be shipped back to the United States at all, and then whether or not the body should be brought home for burial or buried in a national cemetery. On the back of the card, the dead soldier's mother wrote: "If there is any remains left when he is supposed to arrive and if you are sure it is our son we want him buried in Menominee."[57]

Had Mrs. Johnson known of Harold Johnson's Report of Disinterment and Reburial in April 1921, she might have decided against bringing her son home. Of course, by the time she would have received the document (in this fantasy scenario), it would have been too late: the report was generated on the same day as Johnson's Report of Disinterment, Preparation, and Shipment of Body. On Johnson's RDR was written a familiar story that seriously challenged Mrs. Johnson's conditions for return of the body to Menominee. The report read: "Body Badly decomposed. Features unrecognizable, skeleton disarticulated . . . Entire lower portion of skull missing. Two small portions of cranium found. Impossible to execute tooth chart [see RDR in Plates section of this book]." Perhaps even more devestating would have been the following: "Disc found on body partially disintegrated by corrosion, inscription visible as follows: 'Harold--- nso--- 263707, body found in grave 91, Sect a. Pt. 2 under grave marker inscribed Jacob Jaworski, Pvt. Co. L. 125th Inf.' Cross bearing inscription Harold Johnson, Sgt. Co. L. 125th Inf. found over Gr 114, Pt.A Sect. 3."[58]

As time passed and they waited for the bodies of husbands and sons to be shipped home, some family members of the Menominee soldiers became increasingly suspicious and even churlish. Lena (Mrs. Oscar) Falk, who had not even received official notification of her husband's death in early-August 1918 until late-October 1918 (see Essay 2), echoed the sentiments of others when she wrote to the Chief of the Graves Registration Service. Her letter to Colonel Charles Pierce must have stung: "*When they bring our men home I want to be sure I have my husband* [her emphasis]. So many mistakes have been made."[59]

The "Burial Case Files" demonstrate just what a lengthy and difficult task the GRS faced. The GRS's problems, in real life and on paper, began with numerous graves dug hastily under battle conditions and were exacerbated through the need to continually "concentrate" graves after the war into fewer and larger cemeteries as dead soldiers were shipped back to the States. As the AEF burgeoned, and to handle the massive logistical problems, the GRS itself grew from a tiny unit of two officers and fifty men to a vast outfit of 7,000 men and 150 officers.[60] While the Burial Case Files are, perhaps, an extreme example of making and keeping records under duress, it is difficult, indeed, to read these records without altering permanently one's view of the nature of record making and record keeping.[61] In an attempt to fulfill a promise, the GRS and Cemeterial Division displayed a strange mix of assiduous record generation and a sort of whimsy — or at least denial — when it came to recognizing (or, perhaps, telling) the truth of the matter: that the identity of many soldiers had been, essentially, confused or lost forever.

And what of John Teichler? The Michigan Historical Commission's *Michigan in the World War: Military and Naval Honors of Michigan Men and Women* notes that Teichler was posthumously awarded the Distinguished Service Cross and Croix de Guerre.[62] The official account of how he earned these medals was not necessarily entirely false, but did not agree with a later eyewitness report of his death. Fittingly, both the eyewitness report and the "official account" from *Michigan in the World War* contradict the Death Affidavit from Teichler's Burial Case File. Still, the body in Teichler's Menominee grave might well be "Teichler," since the eyewitness account of Teichler's death squares with information in his file's RDRs. The eyewitness, Corporal John C. Daley of Company L, told The *Herald-Leader* that Teichler had been wounded and was moving to the rear when he bent down to care for another wounded soldier. Daley said that Teichler had been hit in the back of the head and killed instantly.[63]

---

[1]Correspondence, Reports, Telegrams, Applications, and Other Papers Relating to Burials of Service Personnel ("Burial Case Files"), 1915-1939; Cemeterial Division; RG 92; NACP. Hereafter cited as "Burial Case Files"; Cemeterial Division; RG 92; NACP.

[2]A concise account of this and the Quartermaster Corps' role in matters related to the burial of soldiers — on the pages cited, from 1775 until World War I — can be found in Sledge, *Soldier Dead*, 36-37. Also, for the formation of the GRS in World War I, see United States Army Quartermaster Corps, "History of the American Graves Registration Service: Q.M.C. in Europe, vol.1," 12-13 and ff. (Hereafter cited as USAQMC, "History of the AGRS," vol. number). "The Graves Registration Service . . . was in March, 1920 merged into the Cemeterial Division of the office of the Quartermaster General," according to USAQMC, "History of the AGRS," Vol. 1, 43.

[3]USAQMC, "History of the AGRS," Vol. 1, 27.

[4]Patrols did cross the Vesle; I am speaking here of sizeable numbers of troops. A summary of operations can be found in CMH, *Order of Battle*, Vol. 2, 182-183. The American Battle Monuments Commission (ABMC) prepared and the Government Printing Office (GPO) produced an excellent source of maps of the major operations in which the American Expeditionary Forces (AEF) fought, including the Aisne-Marne campaign and others; now out-of-print, but still fairly easy to obtain, *American Armies and Battlefields in Europe* includes large, fold-out maps (placed in a pocket in the back of the book) that show where the front lines were on any given day. I estimated the miles gained using the large (27 1/4 x 31 1/2") map entitled "American Operations in the Aisne-Marne Region, May 31-October 12, 1918." This book also identifies and pictures locations of the permanent American cemeteries in the between-wars period, one of which (the Oise-Aisne American Cemetery at Seringes-et-Nesles) holds, among the many soldiers buried there, what were identified as the remains of Anton and Albert Johnson; map attached, 103.

[5]United States, *Field Service Regulations: United States Army*, 158. You may notice that the GRS was thus operating under the dual authority of U.S. Army commanders and the Chief, Graves Registration Service. Sledge, *Soldier Dead*, 191.

[6]USAQMC, "History of the AGRS," vol. 1, 5.

[7]Ibid., 13-14.

[8]Ibid., 19. I believe that such blanks may appear in these files. I call them Grave Location Forms in this essay; the format of the document changed over time. It is possible that they were not filled out "at once"; at least I did not see that. They were, however, filled out repeatedly as circumstances warranted.

[9]Ibid., 15, 103. This figure — 73,000 — sounds like, and is, a large number of casualties (and, in a very short time—200 days of fighting). But one must remember, to put this figure in perspective, that as John Keegan puts it, "the names of those who had been lost altogether were inscribed on architectural monuments, the largest of which, at Thiepval, records the names of the 70,000 *missing* [my emphasis] of the battle of the Somme"; *Keegan, First World War*, 422.

[10]USAQMC, "History of the AGRS," vol. 1, 4.

[11]Ibid., 7.

[12]Report of Death, July 15, 1919; Faber, Arthur, file folder not numbered; NM-81, E-1942, NWCH, HMFY 2000; "Burial Case Files," Cemeterial Division; RG 92; NACP. The "direct cause of death" was recorded on this form as "suicide by hanging," but death "was" listed as being "in line of duty" and not as "the result of the deceased's own willful misconduct." I am not sure what to make of that. The Herald-Leader Company, *Honor Roll of Menominee County*, 57, asserted that he "died from injuries received overseas." According to the "Report of Death" in Faber's file, the "Nature of injury or disease" that Faber had suffered from was termed "psychoneurosis, psychasthenia." The headstone on his grave reads: "Died . . . of injuries received in the line of duty in France." Of course, this was true as metaphor only but true nonetheless. Falk makes several appearances in the text of this book. See, for example, Essay 1, pages 5-6.

[13]Death Affidavit; Teichler, John, file folder not numbered; NM-81, E-1942, HMFY 2000; "Burial Case Files"; Cemeterial Division; RG 92; NACP. Hereafter cited as Teichler, John; "Burial Case Files"; RG 92; NACP. Time of death was given in these Death Affidavits as 3:30 P.M. for three of the nine soldiers from Company L killed on July 31.

[14]A typical addition, but not, strictly speaking, part of this form, though incorporated into later versions.

[15]Report of Disinterment and Reburial (One), June 13, 1919; Teichler, John; "Burial Case Files"; Cemeterial Division; RG 92; NACP.

[16]Document form in the Burial Case Files appeared increasingly more "standardized" as the years passed.

[17]Grave Location Form, July 3, 1919; Teichler, John; "Burial Case Files"; Cemeterial Division; RG 92; NACP. Some relatives of deceased soldiers lived in Europe; this might be what "European Address" means.

[18]Report of Disinterment and Reburial (Two), December 8, 1920; Teichler, John; "Burial Case Files"; Cemeterial Division; RG 92; NACP.

[19]Report of Disinterment and Reburial (One), June 13, 1919; Teichler, John; "Burial Case Files"; Cemeterial Division; RG 92; NACP.

[20]Report of Disinterment and Reburial (Two), December 8, 1920; Teichler, John; "Burial Case Files"; Cemeterial Division; RG 92; NACP.

[21]Case of Private David T. Davis; Teichler, John; "Burial Case Files"; Cemeterial Division; RG 92; NACP. The Davis case also contains one unnamed finding, similar to an indorsement.

[22]Request for Disinterment, October 9, 1920, Case of Private David T. Davis; Teichler, John; "Burial Case Files"; Cemeterial Division; RG 92; NACP.

[23]2nd Indorsement, December 10, 1920, Case of Private David T. Davis; Teichler, John; "Burial Case Files"; Cemeterial Division; RG 92; NACP.

[24]3rd Indorsement, January 6, 1921, Case of Private David T. Davis; Teichler, John; "Burial Case Files"; Cemeterial Division; RG 92; NACP.

[25]4th Indorsement, January 12, 1921, Case of Private David T. Davis; Teichler, John; "Burial Case Files"; Cemeterial Division; RG 92; NACP.

[26]Information Sheet, March 10, 1921; Teichler, John; "Burial Case Files"; Cemeterial Division; RG 92; NACP.

[27]Identification Opinion, March 12, 1921; Teichler, John; "Burial Case Files"; Cemeterial Division; RG 92; NACP.

[28]Report of Disinterment and Reburial (Three), May 10, 1921; Teichler, John; "Burial Case Files"; Cemeterial Division; RG 92; NACP.

[29]Ibid.

[30]5th Indorsement, January 24, 1921, Case of Private David T. Davis; Teichler, John; "Burial Case Files"; Cemeterial Division; RG 92, NACP. 7th Indorsement, February 12, 1921, Case of Private David T. Davis; Teichler, John; "Burial Case Files"; Cemeterial Division; RG 92; NACP. 8th Indorsement, May 14, 1921, Case of Private David T. Davis; Teichler, John; "Burial Case Files"; Cemeterial Division; RG 92; NACP. Report of Disinterment and Reburial (Three), May 10, 1921; Teichler, John; "Burial Case Files"; Cemeterial Division; RG 92; NACP. David Davis' body was found — apparently. In Februrary 1921, the 7th Indorsement in the Davis case listed Grave 211, Section F, Plot 5 as belonging to an "unknown" soldier; by May that grave was said in the 8th Indorsement to be that of Davis. The 5th Indorsement records Henry Grashoff's body as "buried between Graves 250 and 251, Plot 5, Sect. H." To one side of Teichler lay the remains of Robert Bannister of Company L, 125th Infantry, according to the 6th Indorsement, although no identification beyond the name on the grave's cross could be made. 6th Indorsement, February 8, 1921, Case of Private David T. Davis; Teichler, John; "Burial Case Files"; Cemeterial Division; RG 92, NACP. According to the 5th Indorsement, to the other side of Grashoff (who was, of course, later reburied), in Grave 251, lay Edward Collins of Company L, 125th Infantry. Bannister, Collins, and, as we know, Teichler, were all killed at Hill 212 on July 31.

[31]Report of Disinterment and Reburial (Four), February 1, 1922; Teichler, John; "Burial Case Files'; Cemeterial Division; RG 92; NACP.

[32]Ibid.

[33]Report of Disinterment, Preparation, and Shipment of Body, February 1, 1922; Teichler, John; "Burial Case Files"; Cemeterial Division; RG 92; NACP.

[34]Ibid. In April 1921, Antwerp became the "sole port of operations and activities with reference to the reception of bodies destined for the United States"; see USAQMC, "History of the AGRS," vol. 2, 75; for use of barges to transport bodies to Antwerp, see chapter IV.

[35]Western Union telegram, March 31, 1922; Teichler, John; "Burial Case Files"; Cemeterial Division; RG 92; NACP.

[36]Receipt of Remains, April 29, 1922; Teichler, John; "Burial Case Files"; Cemeterial Division; RG 92; NACP.

[37]State of Michigan, Registrar's Permit for Burial or Removal, April 29, 1922; Riverside Cemetery, Menominee, Michigan.

[38]Report of Disinterment, Preparation, and Shipment of Body, May 11, 1921; St. Peter, Fred, file folder not numbered; NM-81, E-1942, HMFY 2000; Burial Case Files"; Cemeterial Division; RG 92; NACP.

[39]Report of Disinterment and Reburial, June 12, 1919; Lueskow, Arthur, file folder not numbered; NM-81, E-1942, NWCH, HMFY 2000; "Burial Case Files"; Cemeterial Division; RG 92; NACP.

[40]Report of Disinterment and Reburial, April 29, 1921; Lueskow, Arthur, file folder not numbered; NM-81, E-1942, NWCH, HMFY 2000; "Burial Case Files"; Cemeterial Division; RG

92; NACP.

[41]Grave Location Form (One), circa late 1918-early 1919; Stauber, John, file folder not numbered, NM-81, E-1942, HMFY 2000; "Burial Case Files"; Cemeterial Division; RG 92; NACP. Hereafter cited as Stauber, John; "Burial Case Files"; Cemeterial Division; RG 92; NACP.

[42]Grave Location Form (Two), circa late 1918-early 1919; Stauber, John; "Burial Case Files"; Cemeterial Division; RG 92; NACP.

[43]Report of Disinterment and Reburial, June 16, 1919; Stauber, John; "Burial Case Files"; Cemeterial Division; RG 92; NACP.

[44]Grave Location Form (Three), July 16, 1919; Stauber, John; "Burial Case Files"; Cemeterial Division; RG 92; NACP.

[45]Case of Private John Stauber, Board of Review findings, June 28, 1921; Stauber, John; "Burial Case Files"; Cemeterial Division; RG 92; NACP.

[46]Case of Unknown U.S. Soldier No. S-82, Board of Review findings, June 28, 1921; Stauber, John; "Burial Case Files"; Cemeterial Division; RG 92; NACP.

[47]Report of Disinterment and Reburial, June 11, 1922; Stauber, John; "Burial Case Files"; Cemeterial Division; RG 92; NACP. Also see Report of Disinterment and Reburial, May 17, 1921 and Report of Disinterment and Reburial, May 20, 1921 in the Stauber file. Of course, this demands the question: since neither the body in Grave 270 nor the body in Grave 274 (nor the body in Grave 272, for that matter) could be identified, why was the body in Grave 270 assigned the identity of Stauber when his body was already recorded as having been buried in Grave 274? This remains a mystery that I could not solve from the remaining records in the Stauber file.

[48]Report of Disinterment and Reburial, May 20, 1921: Stauber, John; "Burial Case Files"; Cemeterial Division; RG 92; NACP.

[49]Report of Disinterment and Reburial, June 16, 1919; Stauber, John; "Burial Case Files"; Cemeterial Division; RG 92; NACP.

[50]Shipping Inquiry, February 11, 1921 (date of issue); Stauber, John; "Burial Case Files"; Cemeterial Division; RG 92; NACP. Compilation of Disposition of Remains Data, 1921-1922; Stauber, John; "Burial Case Files"; Cemeterial Division; RG 92; NACP.

[51]Captain Charles J. Wynne, Office of the Quartermaster General (Cemeterial Division), to Mr. Michael Stauber, December 14, 1921; Stauber, John; "Burial Case Files"; Cemeterial Division; RG 92; NACP.

[52]Information Sheet, undated [stamped, September 15, 1921]; Stauber, John; "Burial Case Files"; Cemeterial Division; RG 92; NACP.

[53]See, for example, Report of Disinterment and Reburial, May 17, 1921 and Report of Disinterment and Reburial, June 11, 1922; Stauber, John; "Burial Case Files"; Cemeterial Division; RG 92; NACP. This is to say that the Army was not very straightforward in their attempt to gather evidence. The letter to Stauber was not about keeping complete records: it was about finding and deciding on the identity of bodies. On another note, the 1919 RDR in Stauber's file is a much more rudimentary form and does not describe the state of the body exhumed.

[54]Michael Stauber to The Quartermaster General's Dep't of the Army, December 21, 1921; Stauber, John; "Burial Case Files"; Cemeterial Division; RG 92; NACP. John Stauber: November 25, 1898-July 31, 1918.

[55]Receipt of Remains, July 16, 1922; Stauber, John; "Burial Case Files"; Cemeterial Division; RG 92; NACP.

[56]Compilation of Disposition of Remains Data, 1921-1922; Stauber, John; "Burial Case Files"; Cemeterial Division; RG 92; NACP.

[57]Request for Burial in the United States, circa December 1920; Johnson, Harold, file folder not numbered; NM-81, E-1942, NWCH, HMFY 2000; "Burial Case Files"; Cemeterial Division; RG 92; NACP.

[58]Report of Disinterment and Reburial, April 13, 1921; Johnson, Harold, file folder not numbered; NM-81, E-1942, NWCH, HMFY 2000; "Burial Case Files"; Cemeterial Division; RG 92; NACP. The evidence shows that a disc on a "body" trumped other factors in making determinations of identification; but, of course, this is still extremely problematic given the circumstances of burial and reburial.

[59]Lena (Mrs. Oscar) Falk to Colonel Charles Pierce, Chief, Graves Registration Service, February 16, 1920; Falk, Oscar Thomas, file folder 72307; NM-81, E-1942, NWCH, HMFY 2000; "Burial Case Files"; Cemeterial Division; RG 92; NACP. The impetus for Lena Falk's writing the Chief of the GRS came from her receiving photographs from the government of the grave of her husband. The grave number on the cross in the pictures, "85," did not match the information she had been given as to where her husband had been buried. The reason for this was that she had not been informed of Oscar Falk's reburial and the location of that grave. Captain Charles Wynne, head of the Inquiry Section of the GRS, then wrote back to Lena Falk and told her where her husband was reburied. Thus, some families must have received photographs of graves upon request (and remember, Oscar Falk was a captain) but it appears from the evidence that they were not necessarly to be informed of reburial locations (as I explain in the text of the essay). Captain Charles J. Wynne, QMC, Graves Registration Service, to Lena (Mrs. Oscar) Falk, February 25, 1920; Falk, Oscar Thomas, file folder 72307; NM-81, E-1942, NWCH, HMFY 2000; "Burial Case Files"; Cemeterial Division; RG 92; NACP. A year earlier, Lena Falk had received a letter from Pierce's office that may partly help explain her frustration: "I'm sorry you did not get this information [the burial site of Oscar Falk in France] ere this. The reason why this office never sent out notification letter (per enclosed), is due to the fact that nearest relative address did not appear on records. Had I thought of looking at the card, this information could have been forwarded months ago. I'm enclosing bulletins which will give you the information desired in regard to the removal of the body [from France to Menominee]. . . . In the meantime, I would like to have a note from you making a definite statement that you wish the Captain's body brought to the United States when conditions warrant such action. Such request will be put on file. I am writing John S. Zelie, chaplain, who had charge of the Captain's burial, to acquaint you regarding circumstances of death. Such information is not on record here. Matter of personal effects has been taken up with the Effects Depot, St. Nazaire. I have asked that they communicate with you direct[ly]." Signature illegible, believed to be Wynne or Pierce, to Lena (Mrs. Oscar) Falk, Februrary 21, 1919; Oscar Falk file; MCHS-ARC.

[60]USAQMC, "History of the AGRS," vol.1, 14.

[61]In this connection see, for example, Pease, "Caution Regarding Military Documents," 282-284, which, just after World War I, discussed the conditions and methods under which military documents were created in wartime and the relative value of these. For helping me to better understand these issues I owe thanks to Eliot Wilczek, Tufts University Archivist, who is currently working on record making and record keeping in World War I.

[62]Landrum, *Michigan in the World War*, 65; 218-219.

[63]"42 Co. L Boys Killed in Five Hours," *HL*, February 5, 1919. A comparison of dental records from the Teichler file's 1921 Information Sheet (see note 26 above for citation) and the Davis/Teichler RDRs shows some slight evidence that the body sent back to Menominee was Teichler, but that evidence is far from conclusive.

Epilogue

Homecoming

On May 30, 1919, Company L came home. Menominee went wild. The *Herald-Leader* traced the return trip: from New York, to Port Huron, to Camp Custer, to Chicago.[1] Finally, only one leg of the journey remained.

On May 28th, the newspaper noted, "They [the soldiers] are expected to arrive in Chicago tomorrow night and will start for home over the Northwestern line at 9 o'clock Friday morning, and if the weather man is generous Menominee will see a demonstration, when the boys arrive, that will be written as the most memorable in the history of this city. At least fifteen thousand people are expected to turn out."[2]

If anything, the intensity of the occasion had increased by the next day. On May 29, the headline read, "Co. L Home Tomorrow at 5:54 p.m." A parade had been scheduled, to be followed by other festivities. "Menominee will rock in tribute," the article announced, "as the khaki-clad boys hop off the train and take their places at the very head of the parade. The procession will move without delay on the line of march from the depot to Ogden, east to Main, thence to Hotel Menominee under banners and the great Victory arch, especially provided for the return of the men of Company L." At the hotel, the soldiers would greet family, friends, sweethearts, be treated to "a fine dinner" — and, in a thoughtful touch for tired soldiers, "with no speeches."[3]

Fifteen area men, including Oliver Allard and Isaac Chandler, along with four other Upper Peninsula soldiers from Company L, finally got off the train in Menominee. The celebration was everything that had been hoped for — and more. "They were home," the local daily intoned. "They were on Ogden avenue and Main street, the dream street, the mirage made real."[4]

Main Street has since been renamed, but present-day First Street, which borders the shores of the Green Bay in Menominee, retains much of its character from the time when Company L returned. One can almost see and hear the ghosts.

What a scene it was. "Menominee yelled its head off," the *Herald-Leader* announced. Bands played, bells rang, whistles blew, girls in white threw flowers beneath the feet of marching soldiers. Red arrows — for the 32nd Division — were everywhere, including the big arch on Main.[5]

The planners of the day's events had worried beforehand about the weather. That Friday was hot, but 17,000 Americans packed the parade route in Menominee. "The crowds were awed, and silent, but a second," reported the *Herald-Leader*, "and then broke into new cheers. They went mad and hoarse and crazed with enthusiasm. . . . Yes, the men in 'L' company found all their dreams come true in Menominee yesterday. . . . It was a wonderful day."[6]

---

[1]"Company L to Reach Here Last of Next Week," *HL*, May 23, 1919; "Company L at Camp Custer," *HL* May 27, 1919.

[2]"Company L Will Reach Home Memorial Day," *HL*, May 28, 1919.

[3]"Co. L Home Tomorrow at 5:54," *HL*, May 29, 1919.

[4]"Menominee Gives Its Heart to Co. L, But What Now?", May 31, 1919.

[5]Ibid.

[6]Ibid.

Afterword

Knowledge exists outside of our not-so-static storehouses — our libraries, archives, and museums — according to Jacques Derrida and John Hunter. "The borders of the human mind or self (or a single corporate entity)," writes Hunter, "are not the borders of memory."[1] It takes imagination, and leaves one "in need of archives"[2] to turn what is there into something that resembles an idea of the truth of the past. This was proven to me as I went back to the Hill 212 battle and looked at fresh sources and as my view of the battle changed over time. The sources — primary sources, archival sources — at one point had led me to believe that Company L had actually surged past Hill 212 and reached, along with other elements of the 3rd Battalion of the 125th Infantry, the objectives set for them in Field Orders No. 11.

This was the memory I generated of what had occurred on July 31, 1918. As I gathered and read other sources, I became convinced that I had erred. And so, Company L's achievement dimmed a bit but settled back to square, in a sense, with the "original" claim in Jeffrey Schultz's display, built in 1981 and housed in Menominee's Heritage Museum, that these soldiers had captured Hill 212. "They" — the 3rd Battalion, 125th Infantry Regiment, and not just L Company — had "captured" (if that is what you want to call it) Hill 212: at least much of it. These same soldiers held Hill 212, too, for most of the next day, which means that they were not advancing. They were pinned down. At least that is what I now imagine based on what I have read and seen. If I had examined but one or two or five sources, my knowledge would have been incomplete. Or more incomplete. The tangled web of sources kept leading me on. It still does, and I have found, as Hunter writes, "that the alien, inhuman quality of knowledge in the world, which the humanists wanted to discipline, is productive and not limiting."[3]

Does all this disillusion, in the dual sense of the word, make these men of Company L more or less heroic than implied in the original Menominee

County Historical Society's Heritage Museum's display?[4] Not at all. The men of Company L killed and were killed. They fought and did not run away. They were surprised in battle and kept fighting. They were inexperienced and gained experience.

One can not help but feel the pathos in the accounts of what happened during that first day of fighting. Take, for example, Lyle Cole's diary from the 3rd Battalion of the 125th Infantry. Cole's account can be humorous at times; for one thing, it shares the seriocomic search for food later made famous in *All Quiet on the Western Front.* But his account of the fight for Hill 212 makes it clear that the battle was a nightmare. At one point, Cole shifts around to speak to his Captain, and thus gets wounded in the foot instead of shot in the head; later, as the bombs come closer and closer to atomizing the wounded soldier, he sullies himself. Writes Cole: "I am not ashamed to say that I cried."[5] Decades later, Oliver Allard still cried as he spoke of the battle to Jeffrey Schultz. One can hardly imagine a more harrowing experience. It is not even a question of heroism; these men required no advertisement for their bravery, but bravery is irrelevant.

My writing has been an attempt to clarify, to remember (piece together) what happened to Company L at Hill 212. Rhetorical questions follow. To those who come to the Heritage Museum and Anuta Archives in Menominee, who know nothing about Company L or Hill 212 or even the difference between World War I and II, what will they learn or remember? What will happen to the memory of Company L, Hill 212, the nine Menominee men from the company killed in action that day, and what would that mean?

---

[1]Hunter, "Minds, Archives," 212-213. This quote is in the context of a discussion of the late sixteenth century critique of an interiority represented in the view of knowledge that had been promulgated in Rome's Golden Age and which the Humanists had taken up in early modern Europe. "The imaginative limits," writes Hunter, "imposed by the *thesaurus* model of memory have prevented us from taking seriously the notion that knowing in all of its valences can be imagined as an interactive process in which knowledge, whether individual or collective, can be located *outside* the body that knows."

[2]Derrida, *Archive Fever*, 91.

[3]Hunter, "Minds, Archives," 213.

[4]The original Heritage Museum display (1981) had slight errors — such as the misspelling of

"Ourcq" (later corrected), the river near Hill 212 — and, perhaps, some errors of emphasis and context, but was a coherent, honest, and intriguing effort that sparked the imagination: mine, for example. Recent versions of this display have partially effaced our memory of the deeds of the Company L soldiers through the inclusion of a patina of unrelated or vaguely related items that generalize and obscure meaning: e.g., an Eisenhower jacket, a Nazi helmet, a picture of a "Rosie the Riveter," items from the Spanish American War. This is the museum display equivalent of a palimpsest. To again invoke Derrida, the display "sweeps away the logic of finitude."

[5]Cole, "1918 Diary," 39.

Bibliography

This bibliography examines sources listed particularly through the lens of *Onward Through Hell*. It includes some sources that may not have been cited or used extensively in *Onward* but that I found helpful in some way. Obviously, the list is by no means exhaustive; in fact, it is idiosyncratic. For this list, I used the edition of the book that I worked with; for example, if I used a paperback, that is the version I cite. In the case of relatively hard-to-find items I noted where I found a copy to use.

Abbreviations in Citations

ABMC	American Battle Monuments Commission
AGRS	American Graves Registration Service
ALIC	Archives Library Information Center, National Archives at College Park, Maryland
CMH	Center of Military History, United States Army
HL	*Menominee Herald-Leader*
JHC	Joint War History Commissions of Michigan and Wisconsin
MCHS-ARC	Menominee County Historical Society Michael J. Anuta Research Center
MHI	Military History Institute, Carlisle, PA
NACP	The National Archives at College Park, Maryland
USAQMC	United States Army Quartermaster Corps

ARCHIVES

Menominee County Historical Society Michael J. Anuta Research Center Menominee, Michigan (MCHS-ARC)

Local history repository.

Documents

Falk collection, including cache of letters, 1916 Company L Muster-In Roll, and documents of the history of the area were all important.

Newspapers

Hard copy of the *Menominee Herald-Leader.*

Photographs

Arresting images including one of a book burning, Oscar Falk in France, and scenes of the celebration readied for Company L's return.

Military History Institute, Carlisle, Pennsylvania (MHI)

Repository of record for military history.

World War I Veterans' Survey, "Army Service Experience Questionnaires."

Very few of these exist from the 125th Infantry Regiment — only eight soldiers participated — and were conducted too late to be of much help, thereby exemplifying the deterioration of memory. Still, some interesting material, particularly that of Joseph M. Donnelly, whose compilation appears in this bibliography and figures in the text of this book.

Reports, diaries, histories

These are listed individually below. One can not do this type of historical work without such sources.

National Archives at College Park (NACP; Record Groups delineated in text by Record Group [RG] number)

World War I primary documents.

Record Group 92, Records of the Office of the Quartermaster General

Cemeterial Division: Correspondence, Reports, Telegrams, Applications, and Other Papers Relating to Burials of Service Personnel ("Burial Case Files").

Information from files for the nine soldiers from Menominee's Company L killed on July 31 plus a few others from Menominee. Fascinating; these records deserved a fuller treatment than I could give them; Essay 3 based on these.

Record Group 407, Records of the Adjutant General's Office

World War I Organization Records; Casualties of AEF by Division.

World War I Strength Returns; Infantry Regiments.

Good for figuring out casualties and strength of hard-hit Company L. July regimental strength report is missing, which is an issue, but one can learn a lot from the August strength report. It isn't pretty.

Record Group 120, Records of the American Expeditionary Forces (World War I)

A.E.F. General Headquarters, G-3 Reports; 32nd Division.

Maps, some of them misleading (as noted in the text) come from these records. "Special reports" — compilation reports on campaigns — and field orders are included in these records.

A.E.F. General Headquarters, War Diaries — (32nd Division).

Has 3rd Battalion war diaries for May, June, and July 1918. War diaries appear reliable, which is not always the case.

World War I Organization Records: 32nd Division, 63rd Infantry Brigade, 126th Infantry Regiment (this includes material on the 125th Infantry), 125th Inf. Rgt.

Operations reports, field messages, and other primary documents for the 125th Infantry and 63rd Brigade.

GOVERNMENT DOCUMENTS

American Battle Monuments Commission (cited as ABMC). *American Armies and Battlefields in Europe: A History, Guide, and Reference Book.* Washington, D.C.: United States Government Printing Office, 1938.

Large color foldout maps showing daily divisional advances and the numerous other maps alone would make this book worthwhile; but the pithy descriptions of battles at the divisional level are excellent and the "tours" of battlefields, cemeteries, and monuments from the late 1930's are interesting. (Author's Collection).

American Battle Monuments Commission. *32nd Division: Summary of Operations in the World War.* Washington, D.C.: United States Government Printing Office, 1943.

A key, highly reliable, source, especially good for figuring out an overview of "what happened," although even this source must be balanced with other information. Terse, accurate, descriptions of battle movements of units down to the battalion level. At times one must read between the lines. Valuable research tool. (ALIC).

Center of Military History, United States Army. *Order of Battle of the United States Land Forces in the World War.* Vol. 2, *American Expeditionary Forces: Divisions.* Washington, D.C.: Center of Military History, 1988.

Standard for composition of units and engagements in which they fought. Copies readily obtained.

Center of Military History, United States Army. *United States Army in the World War 1917-1919.* Vol. 5, *Military Operations of the American Expeditionary Forces.* Washington, D.C.: Center of Military History, 1988.

Monumental and indispensable work on the war, also available in CD-ROM. For purposes of this book, I used this source to understand more about the forces opposing Company L and the 32nd Division: used for translated orders that discern the Germans' intent to retreat from the Ourcq to the Vesle; also useful for identification of units that the 32nd Division fought against. (ALIC).

United States; War Department. *Field Service Regulations: United States Army, 1914, Corrected to January 15, 1918 (Changes Nos. 1 to 8).* Washington, D.C.: Government Printing Office, 1918.

Regulations include those for care of dead soldiers under "Sanitary Service." (Author's Collection).

ARTICLES, BOOKS, MANUSCRIPTS, FILMS, NEWSPAPER

Allard, Oliver. "Sixty Years Ago Co. L Men Faced German Machine Gun Fire on Hill 212." Typescript.

Belated account, with the candid if somewhat veiled war memories of a very fine person; Allard truly was an officer and a gentleman. A sergeant with Company L on July 31, Allard was eventually promoted on the field to second lieutenant, one of only fifteen soldiers from the 125th Infantry to be commissioned from the ranks without first attending an officers' training school. Focus is on the battle near Chateau-Thierry and thus extremely useful. (Personal Collection of Jeffrey Schultz).

Alexander, Robert. *Memories of the World War: 1917-1918.* New York: MacMillan, 1931.

Alexander assumed command of the 63rd Brigade of the 32nd Division (Company L's brigade) on August 5 during the march from the Ourcq to the Vesle. Ill-treated upon his arrival at the 32nd Division at the hands of Major General William Haan, Alexander was soon promoted and transferred to command of the 77th Division. Alexander's account exonerates his predecessor, General William Conner. It is well that Alexander does so, because General Robert Lee Bullard's account (see below) speaks of a brigadier who lost his brigade because he failed to follow orders from the French; all of the particulars in Bullard's account do not appear to fit Conner's case or that of the 63rd, but there is enough there to raise doubt. As a researcher, I ran into many statements about Conner similar to Alexander's and I have asked myself why everyone is so careful not to slight Conner since, obviously, being replaced in the middle of a campaign can raise red flags. On the other hand, the AEF had a habit of pulling officers away from their commands at the most awkward of moments (notably, this was done just prior to the Meuse-Argonne offensive with predictable results).

Allen, Hervey. *Toward the Flame: A Memoir of World War I.* Lincoln: University of Nebraska Press, 2003.

Originally published in the 1920s, revised in the 1930s, and had not been reprinted since 1968 (Lengel). Arguably the best published American memoir on World War I. Allen, a lieutenant in the 28th Division (also originally a National Guard unit), recounts the Drive from the Ourcq to the Vesle and the brutal fighting around Fismes and Fismette on the Vesle. The 28th Division followed the 32nd Division and on August 6-7 relieved the 32nd (and Company L) on the drive to the Vesle. Not much that helped directly with *Onward* (the July 31 battle part, anyway), but absolutely essential: both intelligent and affecting. Tone alternates between surreal idyllic beauty (as in the 90s film, *The Thin Red Line*) and surreal gritty street fighting (urban scenes reminiscent of Kubrick's *Full Metal Jacket*). In a preface to the 1934 edition, Allen said he ended the book, "when the film burned out." A counter to woofing about the glory of war, but not preachy. Allen wrote this memoir as an antidote for haunted sleep.

Audoin-Rouzeau, Stephane and Annette Becker. *14 — 18: Understanding the Great War.* New York: Hill and Wang, 2003.

A tour-de-force. Useful for the French/Allied view of the Germans and vice versa. Freud makes another appearance.

Brannen, Carl Andrew. *Over There: A Marine in the Great War.* College Station: Texas A&M UP, 1996.

This source is a good example of the many accounts that speak of harrowing isolation on the battlefield. Background, but linked to the persistent idea in Menominee that Company L captured Hill 212 single-handedly.

Braun, John A. *Together in Christ: A History of the Wisconsin Evangelical Lutheran Synod.* Milwaukee: Northwestern Publishing House, 2000.

Used for information on the Lutheran church and German American cultural identity in World War I.

Bruce, Robert B. *A Fraternity of Arms: America and France in the Great War.* Lawrence: University Press of Kansas, 2003.

Asserts that the Aisne-Marne battle was the turning point in World War I.

Bullard, Robert Lee. *Personalities and Reminiscences of the War.* Garden City: Doubleday, 1925. (Author's Collection).

Bullard commanded the III Corps during the Aisne-Marne battle and later the Second Army. Valuable but not particularly frank; at one point he mentions that a brigadier lost his brigade for failing to follow ever-changing orders from the French, under whom Bullard and his men were serving at the time. Bullard apparently wanted to protect the brigadier in question by not naming him, but in so doing he raised suspicions (at least mine) about the commander of the 63rd Brigade, William Conner, who was re-assigned during the campaign. Bullard is more straightforward about the ill-advised action at Fismes and Fismette that followed on the heels of the "Drive from the Ourcq to the Vesle." His account of this action is repeated in Hervey Allen's *Toward the Flame.*

Cole, Lyle S. "A 1918 Diary of World War I and a Condensed History of the 32nd Division." Typescript.

Brief and raw but powerful account of the battle for Hill 212 on July 31. Cole was a sergeant in Company I, in the same battalion as Company L, and was wounded in action. Another example of the war fought almost single-handedly; similar in that respect to the Brannen book. Gallows humor in this and leitmotif of food scrounging that Remarque later made famous. (MHI).

Derrida, Jacques. *Archive Fever: A Freudian Impression.* Translated by Eric Prenowitz. Chicago: University of Chicago Press, 1996.

Laugh this off if you want to. To do so would be a mistake. Postmodernism came late to the professional archival community and, to many intellectuals, Freud is a joke. Evidence that Derrida is right: the Menominee book burning; the partial effacement of the Company L display at the Menominee County Historical Society's Heritage Museum (not discussed at length in this book), while maintaining archival records of the burning and Company L; the recent reclassification of documents at NARA. There are two faces to the fever: one is conservative, essentially, and the compulsion to gather and protect. The other is utterly destructive of memory.

Donnelly, Joseph M., compiler. "A History of Company 'G', 125th Infantry, 32nd Division, World War I." Houghton, MI: 1973. Typescript.

One of the finest sources available for this study and a fascinating read. Captain Donnelly, a law school graduate of the University of Michigan and resident of Michigan's Upper Peninsula, compiled the history decades later, but much of the material was written during the war by Donnelly and previous company commanders, Captains Merritt Lamb (KIA, Aug. 29, 1918) and Elmer Theriault. Donnelly took command of the company on August 14, 1918 and kept a lucid account of the action until he was severely wounded on October 9 in the Meuse-Argonne offensive. After this, only rudimentary notes were kept. G Company was in the 2nd Battalion of the 125th, and thus not in the same battalion as Company L, but the chaos of July 31 and ensuing days is apparent. Menominee's Oscar Falk and Merritt Wilson figure in the history. Donnelly's tale of standing between his battalion commander and a lieutenant while poring over a map at the front during the Meuse-Argonne campaign is a classic; the other two soldiers were wearing the long coats of officers and were shot simultaneously. The absence of page numbers in the copy of the typescript was problematic; chapters are cited within the thesis instead of pages as a result. (MHI).

Ferguson, Niall. *The Pity of War.* New York: Basic, 1999.

Counter-interpretive and provocative. Especially useful for Ferguson's thinking concerning surrenders, and why men fought.

Gansser, Emil. *History of The 126th Infantry in the War with Germany.* Grand Rapids, MI: 126th Infantry Association, A.E.F., 1920.

Excellent regimental history from the other regiment in the 32nd Division's 63rd Brigade (Menominee's Company L was in the 125th). Topographical maps are a welcome addition and shed light on the July 31 action. Gansser's narrative reinforces many of the theories in the Essay 1 material on Menominee's first day in battle. Relatively scarce book. Gansser also co-authored a memoir written in the form of a novel entitled *On the Battle Fields of France in 1918* (see Lengel). (Author's Collection).

Heckel, Edward G., compiler. "History of the 125th Michigan Infantry: Thirty-second Division, 1917, 1918, 1919." Typescript.

Heckel succeeded to command of the 125th during the Oise-Aisne campaign when Colonel William Morrow was wounded on August 29. On September 17, Morrow was relieved of his command; Heckel was promoted to Colonel and commanded the regiment for the remainder of the war. A true compilation; not enough material from any single author or, with due respect, guiding intelligence. A trifle disappointing for the Aisne-Marne offensive. Still, some fine anecdotes and important information on how far the 3rd Battalion made it during the battle for Hill 212. Good, too, on regimental organization, although battalion commanders for the Aisne-Marne battle were only mentioned in passing. One copy available worldwide according to WorldCat. (Michigan Technological University Archives).

The Herald-Leader Company. *The Honor Roll of Menominee County Michigan in the World War: 1917-1918-1919.* Menominee, MI: The Herald-Leader Company, 1921.

A core source, with service biographies and photographs of those who served in the war. Information needs to be verified, but useful and evocative. (Author's Collection).

Hunter, John. "Minds, Archives, and the Domestication of Knowledge." In *Lost in the Archives*, edited by Rebecca Comay, 199-215. Toronto, ON: Alphabet City Media, 2002.

Locates knowledge on the outside. Golden Age of Rome, early modern Europe stressed the thesaurus memory as the fount of knowledge. Cartesian thought disparaged memory and replaced it with reason, but knowledge was still thought to be located within.

Joint War History Commissions of Michigan and Wisconsin. *The 32nd Division in the World War.* Madison: Wisconsin War History Commission, 1920.

Contains photographs of commanders and also photographs of officers killed in the war; lists men killed. For these reasons, the source is excellent. Some say members of the "whine crowd" have slanted history with their pessimism and ironic tone. As historical narrative, this source is the polar opposite: it goes too far in its sunny view and inaccurate glosses. Division's advance shown in map of Aisne-Marne battle, probably derived from contemporary sources, is also optimistic. (Author's Collection).

Keegan, John. *The First World War.* New York: Knopf, 1999.

Standard history of the war and counterpoint to Ferguson.

Kilar, Jeremy W. *Germans in Michigan.* East Lansing: Michigan State University Press, 2002.

Provides background for Essay 2. Good concise history on an immigrant group in the United States. The war placed German Americans under great pressure. Between the war itself and the economic impact of Prohibition, the Germans lost their former "cultural identity."

Kubrick, Stanley, director. *Paths of Glory.* DVD. Santa Monica, CA: MGM Home Entertainment, 1957; 1999.

Watched for "inspiration," if that's what you want to call it. Tightly constructed film. Kirk Douglas is terrific as the Colonel of a French regiment who must obey orders to carry out a suicidal assault. Many of his men can not and do not even depart the trenches, George Macready as Douglas's superior orders the artillery to fire on his own men, and the search for scapegoats begins. Adolphe Menjou plays the cheerful, jaded General who pulls the strings.

Landrum, Charles H., compiler. Edited by George N. Fuller. *Michigan in the World War: Military Honors of Michigan Men and Women.* Lansing, MI: The Michigan Historical Commission, 1924.

Lists Michigan recipients of United States and foreign decorations.

Lanham, C.T., editor. *Infantry in Battle.* Washington, D.C.: The Infantry Journal, Incorporated, 1939.

The introduction to this book states: "By the use of numerous historical examples [from World War I], the reader is acquainted with the realities of war and the extremely difficult and disconcerting conditions under which tactical problems must be solved in the face of the enemy." Chapter X includes an example of an attack of the 3rd Battalion of the 47th Infantry (attached to the 42nd [Rainbow] Division's 168th Infantry). The action takes place near Sergy on July 29th — just two days before Company L attacked. Some American troops even "seemed to be on the south slopes of Hill 212." The caption under the chapter title reads: "A unit must be engaged in accordance with a definite plan. It must not be permitted to drift aimlessly into battle" (138). Obviously, that is exactly what happened, time and again. (Author's Collection).

Lengel, Edward G. *World War I Memories: An Annotated Bibliography of Personal Accounts Published in English Since 1919.* Lanham, MD: Scarecrow Press, 2004.

Fine resource on published personal accounts from World War I. This work was supported through a Military History Institute-affiliated grant. Lengel dismisses Robert Graves and takes an ill-concealed swipe or two at Paul Fussell and his ilk.

Mamet, David. *Three Uses of the Knife: On the Nature and Purpose of Drama.* New York: Vintage, 2000.

Great book. Used in Essay 2 for a change of pace.

McIntosh, Robert. "The Great War, Archives, and Modern Memory." *Archivaria* 46 (Fall 1998): 1-31.

Erodes the notion that archival records are the charge of dispassionate practitioners or the product of "survival of the fittest." The Canadian War Records Office (CWRO) falsified records and created records that functioned as wartime propaganda.

Menne, Edward P. "Diary of a Doughboy." Edited by Jeanne Kosmoski. Typescript.

Menne served in the 121st Field Artillery Regiment, 32nd Division. Nothing of note about July 31 but some interesting comments on "The Drive from the Ourcq to the Vesle" in ensuing days. Very good on the weather (awful), exhaustion, trying to keep pace with the advance, and so forth. (MHI).

Menominee Herald-Leader

Daily newspaper, an important historical source for the Hill 212 affair and the predominant one for Essay 2 on patriotism and propaganda. For today's reader, much irony springs forth from these pages, but the paper shows the build-up of tensions in Menominee over time. National and international news dominated the front pages, a nice precedent no longer followed in many local newspapers, and kept readers abreast of the fighting. Indispensable for descriptions of Company L's return to Menominee and for cultural backdrop; for example, Lillian Gish starred at the local cinema in the summer of 1918. (Spies Public Library, Menominee [on microfilm], and MCHS-ARC).

Morrow, John H., Jr. *The Great War: An Imperial History.* London: Routledge, 2004.

A World War I history for the rest of the world beyond the Western Front. Good for perspective. An example: "Poor Little Belgium, " whose "rape" by Germany fed Allied propaganda "depopulated the Congo by half, from some 20 million to 10 million people" between 1880 and 1920 (8). Also, I am an unabashed believer in the statement Morrow makes in his preface directed at "any who would resort to war or threat of war heedlessly . . . and who would then cloak the enterprise of war in the arrogant, triumphal, and simplistic language of good and evil."

Nenninger, Timothy K. "Tactical Dysfunction in the AEF, 1917-1918." *Military Affairs*, 51, No. 4 (October, 1987): 177-181.

Deep background from National Archives expert. Haunting line: "The Americans had advanced in steady lines across open wheat fields as German machine-gunners shot them down" (178). Sound familiar? This was not the Battle for Hill 212 that Nenninger was describing but might have been. Writes Nenninger: "Rigid plans of attack, lines of infantry advancing over open ground without regard for concealment or cover, little use of fire and maneuver, and improper employment of infantry supporting arms, were typical of American offensives through much of the Summer and Fall of 1918" (178). Thus, Nenninger describes the situation that Company L endured, but also shows that Company L's plight was common.

Pease, Theodore Calvin. "A Caution Regarding Military Documents." *The American Historical Review*, 26, No. 2 (Jan., 1921): 282-284.

See Essay 1. Pease concludes that military documents are often flawed and the historian should rely on eyewitness diaries or letters as a correction.

Persico, Joseph E. *Eleventh Month, Eleventh Day, Eleventh Hour: Armistice Day, 1918; World War I and Its Violent Climax.* New York: Random House, 2004.

Not a lot new in this, but does focus attention on what various units, including the 32nd Division, were doing on the final day of the war and the ambiguous dilemmas units faced.

Reardon, Carol. *Pickett's Charge in History and Memory.* Chapel Hill: University of North Carolina Press, 1997.

A model book on history and memory, on the difficult if not impossible task of discerning what happened during the chaos of battle. Deep background for my thesis and book.

Renoir, Jean, director. *Grand Illusion [La Grande Illusion].* DVD. Criterion Collection: 1937; 1999.

One of the great films ever made. Erich von Stroheim plays the commandant of a prisoner of war camp. His character reminds me of the senior German officers for whom the use of poison gas was anathema.

Scharmach, Sylvia. *Les Terribles.* New York: Pageant Press, 1967.

Contains the diary of Scharmach's uncle, Edward Paikowski, a medic and ambulance driver with Ambulance Company 125 of the 32nd Division. Some riveting tales, but not very useful for the Aisne-Marne campaign because action is condensed, generalized, and few dates are mentioned; better on later campaigns. This source misleads when it wanders from personal anecdote, but in doing so shows what some soldiers *believed.* Added quoted material toward the end of the book mars this work: Frank Simond's egregious account of "the battle of Chateau-Thierry" is reminiscent of some of the more sarcastic lines in Preston Sturges's *Hail the Conquering Hero.* (University of Wisconsin-Oshkosh).

Schmidt, Paul W. *Co. C, 127th Infantry, in the World War.* Sheboygan, WI: Press Publishing Co., 1919.

Captain Schmidt, commander of Company C in the 127th Infantry, 64th Brigade, 32nd Division, gave an extremely candid if somewhat confusing account of facing the German machine guns on the hills and woods near Cierges and Sergy. Valuable company history. (Author's Collection).

Sledge, Michael. *Soldier Dead: How We Recover, Identify, Bury, and Honor Our Military Fallen.* New York: Columbia University Press, 2005.

Excellent work on the Graves Registration Service and successors and a key source for Essay 3. I could not find key WWI archival sources that he used in the limited time I spent at NACP.

Stearns, Gustav. *From Army Camps and Battle Fields.* Minneapolis: Augsburg Publishing House, 1919.

Stearns was Chaplain of the 127th Infantry. This book comprises letters that he wrote to his congregation in Milwaukee, and thus some facts that might have been conveyed would not have passed the censor. Still, a good source in general, and for the Aisne-Marne battle a brief but interesting passage on burying the dead while under fire. (Author's Collection).

Strachan, Hew. *The First World War.* New York: Penguin, 2004.

Strachan is currently writing an exhaustive (the first volume is subtitled *To Arms* and is 1227 pages long) unfinished multivolume work on World War I. By his standards a mere wisp of a book at 364 pages, this is a learned survey with a surprising bonus: a number of colored photographs.

Trask, David. "The Entry of the USA into the War and its Effects." In *The Oxford Illustrated History of the First World War,* edited by Hew Strachan, 239-252. Oxford: Oxford University Press, 1998.

Places the American contribution to Allied victory in perspective.

Travers, Tim. "The Allied Victories, 1918." In *The Oxford Illustrated History of the First World War,* edited by Hew Strachan, 278-290. Oxford: Oxford University Press, 1998.

Fine essay on the turning of the war. Detailed and dense and at the same time easy to understand: quite a feat.

United States Army Quartermaster Corps. "History of the American Graves Registration Service: Q.M.C. in Europe." Consolidated reprint of Vol. 1-3. Washington, D.C.: Office of the Quartermaster General, 1922?. Typescript.

I relied on this source heavily for Essay 3. Takes one through every step of the burial, reburial, and, fascinatingly, the shipping process. (MHI).

United States Army 32nd Infantry Division. "Report on Operations of the Thirty-Second Division, July 29-August 7, 1918 Inclusive: Second Battle of the Marne, 1918." Typescript.

Typical report. Must be viewed with caution as this contains inevitable servings of revisionist history, but also some helpful primary information and commentary. Also available (and used by author) as archival document at NACP. (MHI).

Winter, Jay and Blaine Baggett. *The Great War and the Shaping of the 20th Century*. New York: Penguin Studio, 1996.

Good general introduction to the war with terrific photographs. Coffee table volume, but sound history.

Appendix

Company L, 125th Infantry: Soldiers Killed, July 31, 1918

officers

Hammond, Charles

enlisted men

Allen, Frank	
Allen, George	
Baker, William	Menominee
Bannister, Robert	
Bartlett, Ellsworth (Bugler)	
Boivin, Peter	Menominee
Branchini, Alfred	
Brzozwski, Jacob	
Collins, Edward A.	
Dargo, Leo	
Draper, Frank	
Fulton, Charles	
Hohn, Joseph	
Johnson, Albert	Menominee
Johnson, Harold	Menominee
Kornas, John	
Lesland, Edgar	
Lueskow, Arthur	Menominee
Lux, Jesse	
Martin, Luce	
Pada, Walter	Menominee
Pagnani, Nicola	
Peterson Matt*	
Schoon, Charles	
Spencer, Frank	
St. Peter, Fred	Menominee
Stauber, John	Menominee
Tasson, Nick	
Teichler, John	Menominee
Thompson, Henry	
Toby, Williard	
Wade, William	
Wilkinson, Harry	
	Total = 33

Overall Total (officers and enlisted men) = 34

*DW Aug. 1, possibly as result of action on July 31, and was included

Derived from JHC, *32nd Division in the World War.*

During the Battle

63rd Brigade troops assemble in wheat fields near Hill 212, August 1, 1918 (NACP)

63rd Brigade troops readying for attack near Hill 212, August 1, 1918 (NACP)

The Aftermath of Battle

Captured German machine gun nest, Hill 212, August 2, 1918 (NACP)

Captured German trench mortar position, Hill 212 area (NACP)

Maps

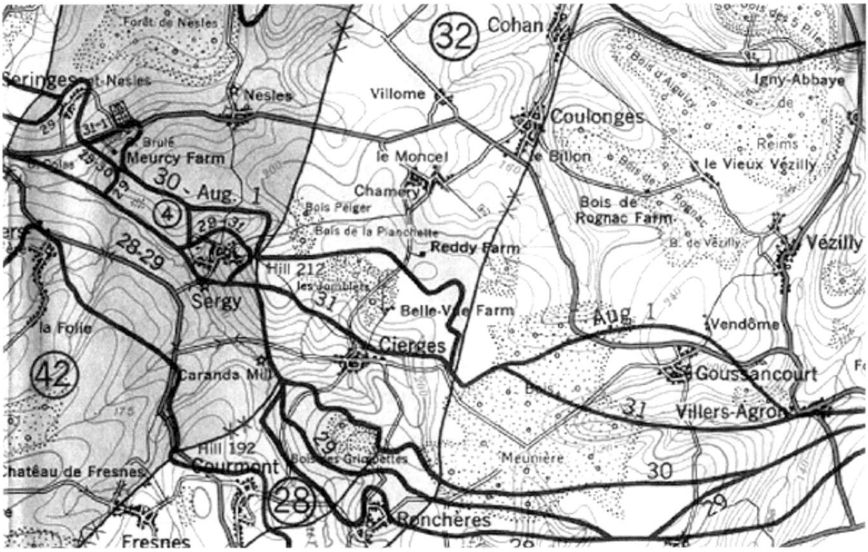

Detail from American Battle Monuments Commission map showing Hill 212 battle area
(see also map, p. 15)

Maps

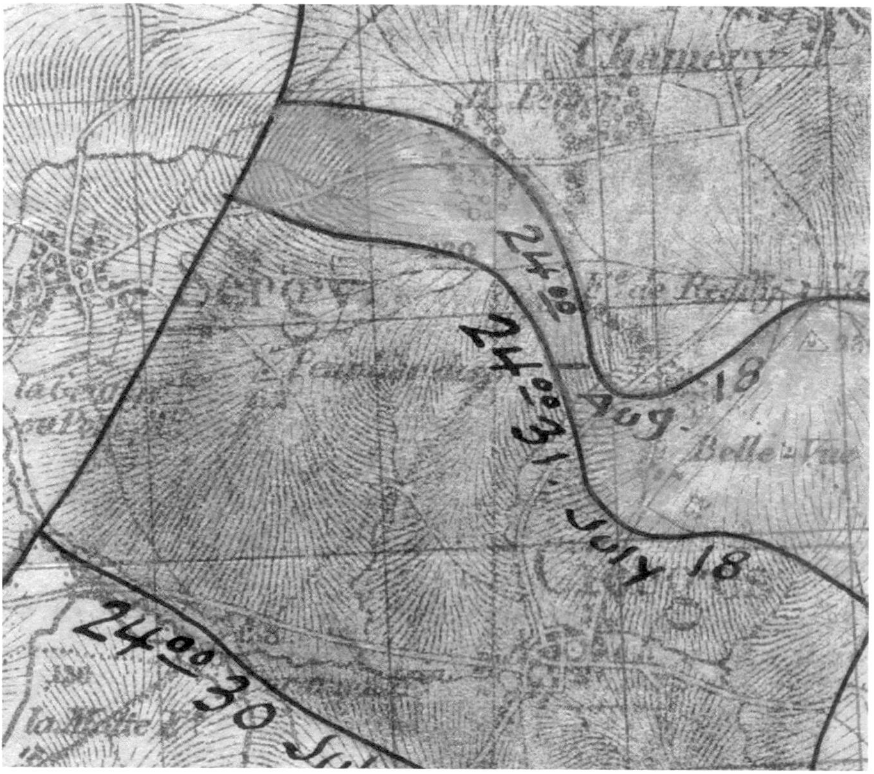

Detail from G-3 map showing battle lines, Hill 212 area; Hill 212 denoted by triangle and dot beneath the "r" and "g" of "Sergy" (NACP)

Maps

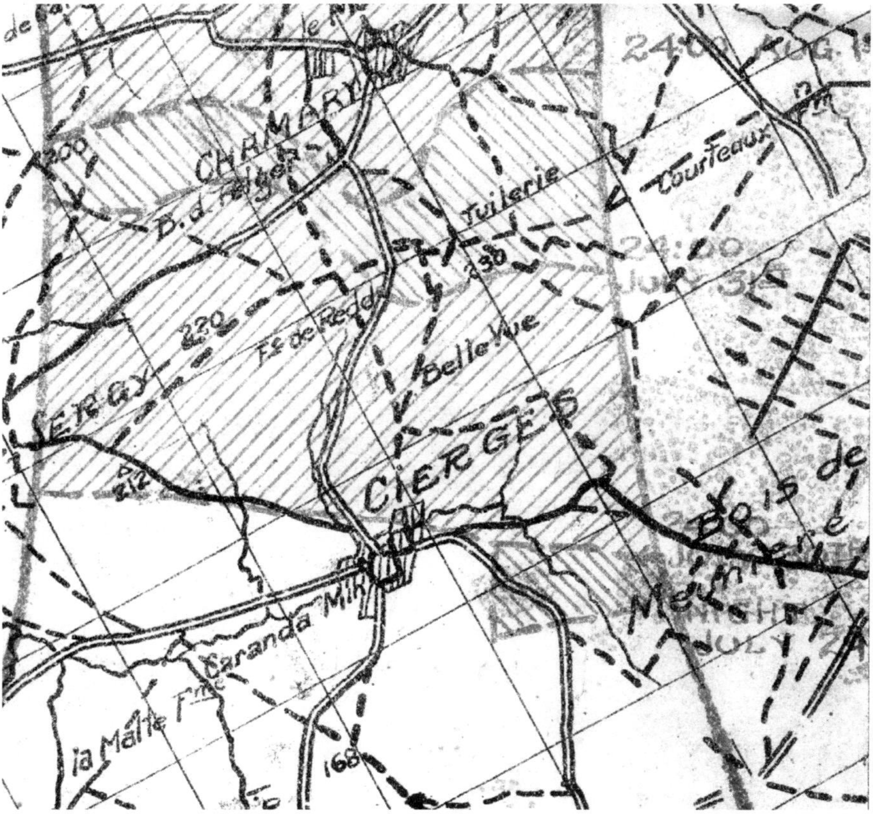

Detail from another C-3 map showing battle lines, Hill 212 area (NACP)

Menominee's Book Burning

Patriotic assembly, June 17, 1918 (MCHS-ARC)

Archives of hell (MCHS-ARC)

The Nine Menominee Soliders from Company L Killed at Hill 212

William Baker

Peter Boivin

Albert Johnson

Harold Johnson

Arthur Lueskow

Walter Pada

Fred St. Peter

John Stauber

John Teichler

From the National Archives "Burial Case Files"

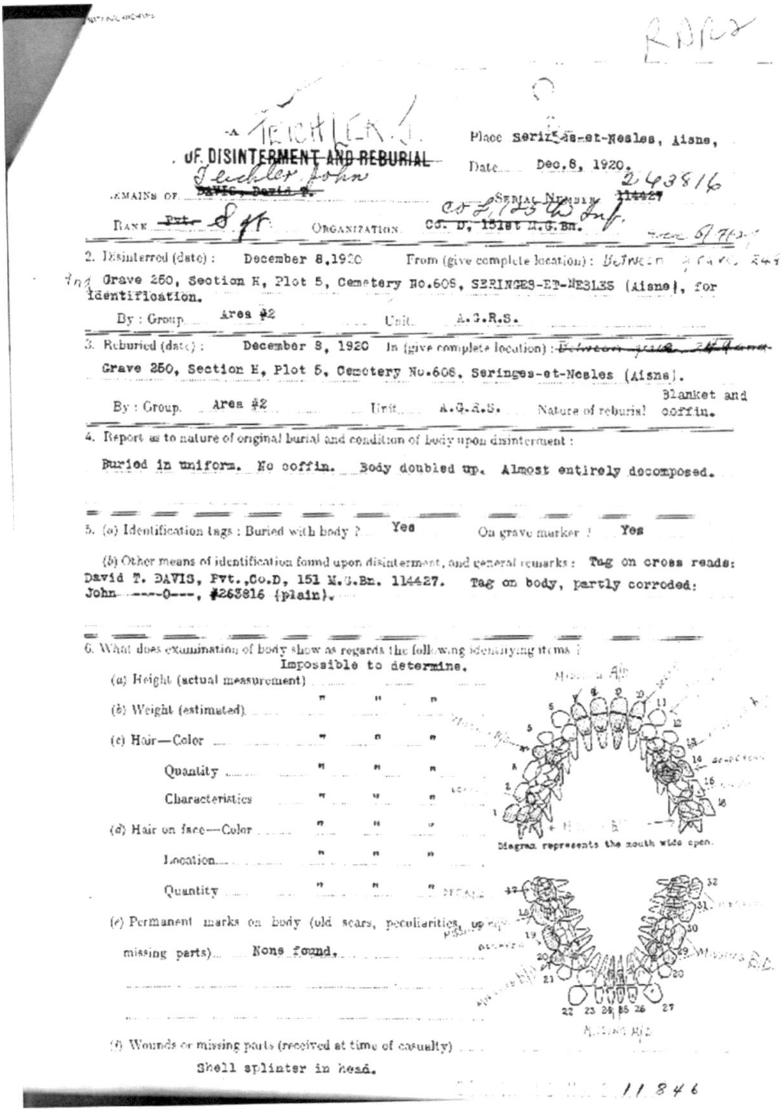

[Teichler J.] ... OF DISINTERMENT AND REBURIAL

Place Serinées-et-Nesles, Aisne,

Date Dec.8, 1920.

REMAINS OF ~~DAVIS, David T.~~ Teichler John

SERIAL NUMBER ~~114427~~ 243816

RANK ~~Pvt.~~ Sgt. ORGANIZATION ~~Co. D, 151st M.G.Bn.~~ Co L, 125 Inf.

2. Disinterred (date): December 8,1920 From (give complete location): Between grave 249 and Grave 250, Section H, Plot 5, Cemetery No.608, SERINGES-ET-NESLES (Aisne), for identification.

By: Group Area #2 Unit A.G.R.S.

3. Reburied (date): December 8, 1920 In (give complete location): ~~Between grave 249 and~~ Grave 250, Section H, Plot 5, Cemetery No.608, Seringes-et-Nesles (Aisne).

By: Group Area #2 Unit A.G.R.S. Nature of reburial Blanket and coffin.

4. Report as to nature of original burial and condition of body upon disinterment:

Buried in uniform. No coffin. Body doubled up. Almost entirely decomposed.

5. (a) Identification tags: Buried with body? Yes On grave marker? Yes

(b) Other means of identification found upon disinterment, and general remarks: Tag on cross reads: David T. DAVIS, Pvt.,Co.D, 151 M.G.Bn. 114427. Tag on body, partly corroded: John ----0---, #263816 (plain).

6. What does examination of body show as regards the following identifying items?

Impossible to determine.

(a) Height (actual measurement) "

(b) Weight (estimated) "

(c) Hair—Color "

Quantity "

Characteristics "

(d) Hair on face—Color "

Location "

Quantity "

(e) Permanent marks on body (old scars, peculiarities, or missing parts) None found.

(f) Wounds or missing parts (received at time of casualty)

Shell splinter in head.

Diagram represents the mouth wide open.

11846

Report of Disinterment and Reburial, John Teichler Burial Case File (NACP)

A Battle Burial Ground

From "History of the American Graves Registration Service: Q.M.C. in Europe"

They Fought at Hill 212

Merritt "Tug" Wilson and Grover Thompson (MCHS-ARC)

Oscar Falk in France (MCHS-ARC)

Company L Comes Home

Preparations for the return of Company L, Menominee, May 1919 (MCHS-ARC)

Victory arch, Main Street, Menominee, May 1919 (MCHS-ARC)

Remembering Company L

Oliver Allard

"Company L in World War I," original display, Heritage Museum, Menominee (MCHS-ARC)